PARIS

Pages 6-7:
When Balzac created the character of Rastignac looking out over the city that he wanted to conquer, he created a dominating vantage-point, that Paris presents today by giving some exceptional points of view. Other than the well-known Eiffel Tower, one can have similar views of the city from the Montparnasse Tower, the Centre Georges-Pompidou, and the Institut du Monde Arabe. There are others places to look out over the city which are more a part of daily life, and which contain relaxing spaces: the terraces of the Samaritaine, Printemps Haussmann, and Galeries Lafayette department stores. There are also several monuments which provide extraordinary views of different neighborhoods in Paris: the top of the Arc de Triomphe de l'Étoile and the towers of the Notre-Dame cathedral. The recently completed Belleville Park, which was created after tearing down a quarter containing old buildings, is a country-like place in the heart of Paris. But the most romantic of these points of view remains the one from the top of the Butte-Montmartre.

Translated from the French by
Kirk McElhearn

Translator's acknowledgments: I would like to thank Marie-France for all her help.
Thanks also to all my friends on Lantra for their help.

Artistic and technical direction:
Ahmed-Chaouki Rafif

Editorial and Iconographic coordination:
Marie-Pierre Kerbrat

Revision:
Geoffrey Finch

© 1999, ACR Édition Internationale, Courbevoie (Paris)
(Art - Création - Réalisation)
© 1999, D.R.
ISBN 2-86770-113-9
N° d'éditeur : 1114/1
Dépôt légal : deuxième trimestre 1999
All rights reserved for all countries.

Printed in France by Mame, Tours.

Jean-Jacques Lévêque

Paris
PLAISIR

ACR Édition

Contents

8	Travelers' Footprints *The boulevard Saint-Michel*
10	A Heart Shaped Island *Lutetia - the île de la Cité*
14	Rome in Paris *The Latin Quarter*
16	Paths of Piety *The Saint-Denis Basilica*
20	Paths of Pilgrims *Saint-Julien, Saint-Séverin and the others*
26	The Stomach of Paris *The "Les Halles" quarter*
32	Le Pré-aux-clercs *Student life, the Sorbonne*
46	From One Palace to Another *The Palais de Justice, the hôtel Saint-Pol, the Louvre, the Tuileries*
56	A Dramatic View *The Champs-Élysées*
62	Swamps and Gossip *The Marais*
70	Squares and Celebrations *From one square to another*
82	The King's Honor *The place des Vosges, the place Dauphine, the hôtel des Invalides*
90	Princely Whims *The Palais-Royal, the Palais de Luxembourg and the large hôtels*
96	Brotherhoods and Watermen *The Hôtel de Ville*
100	The Taking of the Bastille *Paris during the French Revolution*
106	Utopias of a Royal Reign *The palaces of the Roi de Rome, the rue de Rivoli and the place de l'Étoile*
112	A Long, Calm River *The Course of the Seine*
130	Romantic Escapades *The Nouvelle-Athènes quarter*
132	Megalomania *Napoléon III and Haussmann*
136	Paris Walks *The Pont-Neuf, the Galerie du Palais, the place Royale and the Boulevards*

144	Fortifications and Empty Land
	The Thiers Fortifications
146	Parks and Gardens
	From the Tuileries garden to the parc Monceau
156	City Gates
	Gates and Arches
162	Stages and Footlights
	The Châtelet theater, the Opera, theaters, music-halls, and circuses
168	Museums of Paris
	The Musée Carnavalet, Musée Cernuschi, Musée Grévin, Musée Guimet and the rest
170	Villages and Groves
	Villa Frochot, Cité Fleurie, Villa Seurat, the Ruche, the Bateau Lavoir...
180	The Underbelly of the City
	The Parvis de Notre-Dame, the remains of the old Louvre, the Catacombs, the sewers, the metro
186	The Butte Montmartre
	Sacré-Cœur, the Moulin de la Galette, the Lapin Agile
198	The Studios of Montparnasse
	La Rotonde, Le Dôme, La Coupole
202	The Bright Lights of Pigalle
	The Élysée-Montmartre, the Moulin Rouge, and the cabarets of today and yesterday
206	Train Stations
	The gare Saint-Lazare and Impressionism, the Orsay Museum...
212	Shopping Arcades
	The galerie Vivienne, the passage des Panoramas, the passage Colbert...
218	Water in the City
	The Arsenal basin, the canal Saint-Martin, the fountains of Paris
236	Gustave Eiffel and his Tower
	Utopian dreams
244	Worth and Company
	The Opéra quarter, the rue de la Paix and the avenue Montaigne
250	The Tastes of Paris
	Le Grand Véfour, Lapérouse, La Tour d'Argent, Maxim's...
256	The Crown Jewels
	The galerie d'Apollon in the Louvre, the place Vendôme...
258	Renovations and Evolutions
	Parisian urbanism today
284	A Crown of Steel and Concrete
	The boulevard périphérique
286	The Snail
	From Versailles to Saint-Germain-en-Laye, the New Cities

Travelers' Footprints

The boulevard Saint-Michel

Ancient maps give more than a bird's eye view of the area they represent, they highlight the rational growth of a city which organized itself around the beating heart of an island. This island is what gave Paris its snail-like shape.

While Paris is not in the center of France, it has long been a crossroads for travelers from all European countries. Its perfect strategic position convinced Clovis to make it the capital of the vast territories he united under the sign of the conquering Franks, and the modest town of Lutetia progressively became Paris.

It was only much later, and after many adventures which unsettled this quiet town, disturbing the daily lives of its inhabitants, that the Capetians established it as the capital.

The city still wears the signs of this crossroads, as if the footsteps of travelers, pilgrims, merchants and artists wore permanent paths on the ground, paths as strong as fate, even if they have sometimes been woven in fancy, and they ripple, twirl, and bend elegantly, following the lay of the land, as if answering mysterious calls or being led along old forgotten routes.

From north to south was the required route for merchants, artists bringing their knowledge, and goldsmiths, architects, gardeners and geographers bringing their skills from Flanders; from east to west was the route for tourists who came from the far horizons of a Europe covered with fabulous fairy-tale castles. The British came from the northwest; at first they were triumphant ironworkers, but they later became traveling ambassadors for the elegance of Paris. Other roads led off in all directions, toward Melun, Meaux, Soissons, Pontoise, Rouen, Dreux and Chartres.

To the south was Caesar's road, which led to Sens and Orléans. This road became so busy that it was widened by adding a second, parallel lane, the inferior road which later became the rue d'Enfer (Hell street, which is now the boulevard Saint-Michel).

These footprints are many and enduring. Streets and paths are like the wrinkles on a face, they show the age of a city and the weight of its experience. This city has been gutted by winds from all directions, internal storms, and dreams of crazy celebrations. The heart of Paris is lyrical and its head is high in the sky, but its feet are firmly rooted in soil that belonged to peasants before becoming a city of merchants, bourgeois and creators. Because of its concentration, and the permanent melanges which have taken place within its walls, it has become an ardent pole of wisdom and power, of wealth and hope.

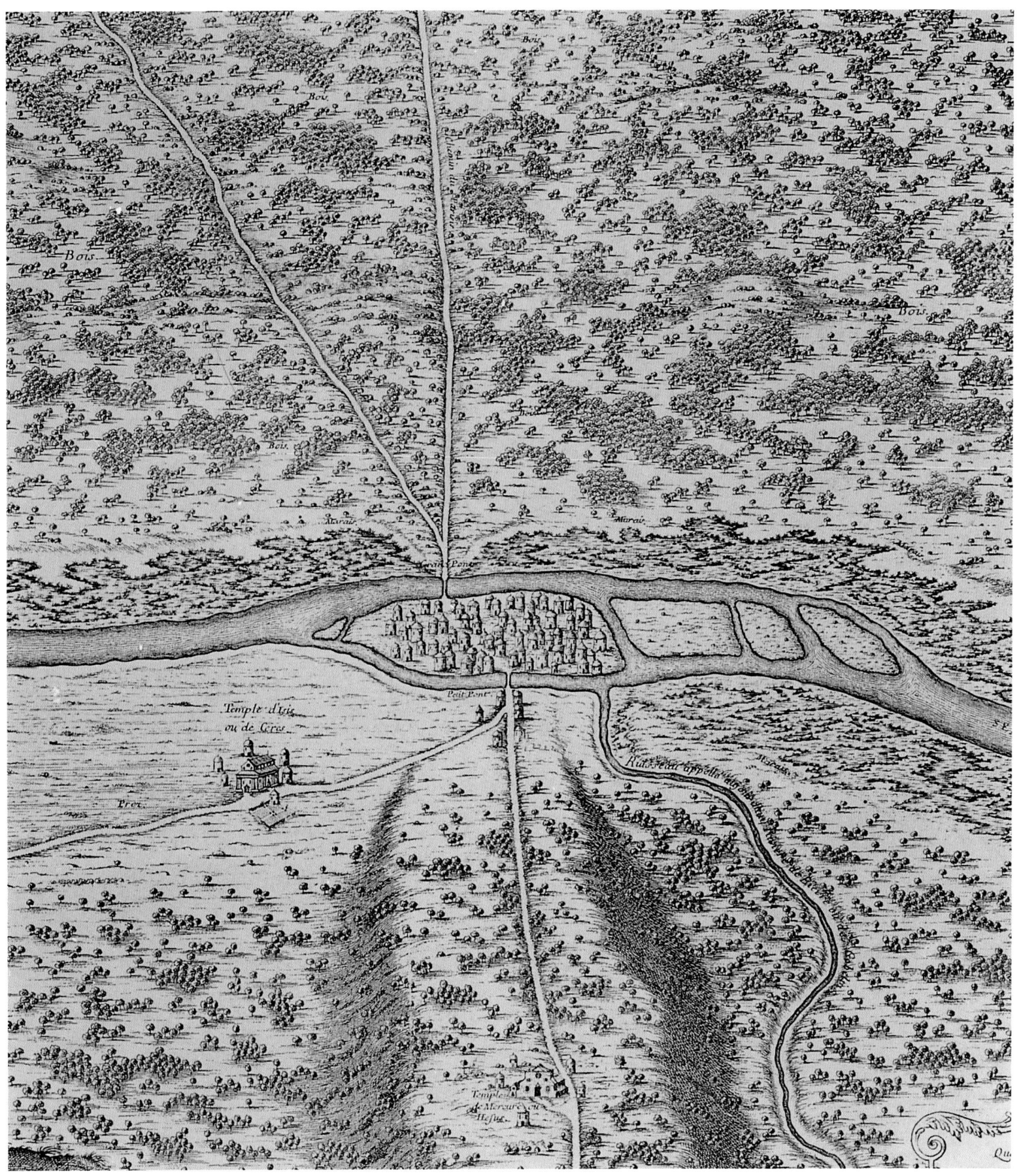

A Heart Shaped Island

Lutetia - the île de la Cité

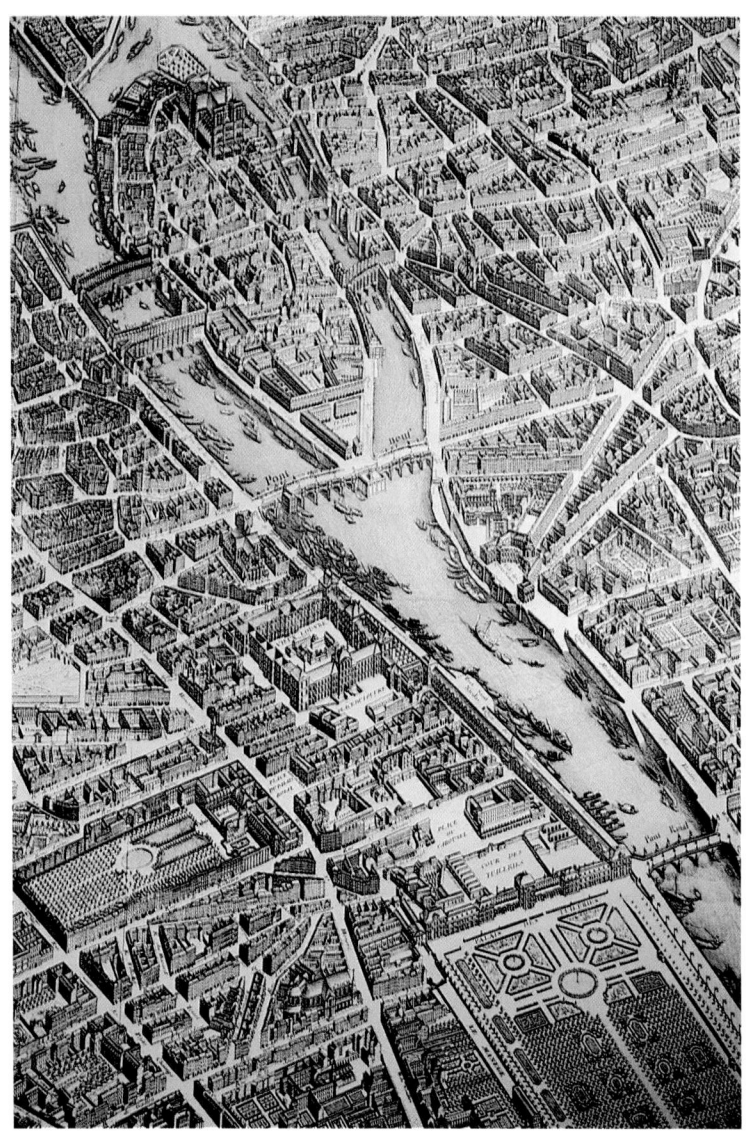

The detailed presentation of all the buildings on the Turgot map is, because of its precision, one of the most valuable documents we have to see exactly how the ancient city was laid out, and what its volume, traffic, and architectural rhythm were like. When looking at this map you become like Gulliver looking over a Paris which has become Lilliput.

The choice of the original site for Paris is justified by the presence of an island, which gave all the guarantees of security that were needed in such a dangerous period. Since then, the appropriately named "île de la Cité" (the Island of the City) has become the traditional center of justice and religion, the two major forces of social life.

Every city needs a legend describing its birth. Paris could not be without one, and even has three of them, which are all rooted in ancient history and the Bible.

We begin in the biblical period. Someone named Dis, who was a descendant of Japhet, the son of Noah, settled in Gaul, and one of his grandsons, Lucus, founded Lutetia. Taking a step forward, to the time of Greek epics, we meet Hercules who, on his way back home from the Danube, with the inhabitants of Parrhasia, stopped over on an enchanted island and decided to settle there: this island is now the île de la Cité. But for the third version, we go on the fiery prose of Homer. One of Priam's grandsons, who had fled from burning Troy, was able to preserve some of the treasures of this legendary city in his refuge in Hungary. One of his descendants, following the courses of different rivers, also landed on this island in the heart and wake of the Seine.

Paris was born from the ships that landed on its banks. In the beginning, the water was also a source of danger. The first chapters in the history of the future capital were punctuated by these passages, which were sometimes brutal and destructive. The grandsons of Troy would have to defend themselves from the sailors who would later come from the north.

But the real history of the Paris we now know began with Caesar, whose envoy, Labiennus, repressed a heroic attempt at resistance by the local population on the Grenelle plain (now the Champ de Mars). Paris was colonized.

The chevet of Notre-Dame, the projecting chapels, located exactly where a pilot-house would be on a boat, highlights the fluvial nature of the site. The surrounding trees and bushes highlight its delicate architecture, and the musical nature of a heavy but gracious upward force, intense yet subtle, in perfect harmony with its surroundings, as if Paris were constructed to resemble its cathedral.

Many great things would come from the often conflicting relations between the Gauls and Romans. Today's France is a child that was raised hearing about the marvelous city of Rome, capital of an empire so huge that it would soon break apart. But France helped pave the way toward the future Europe of monuments, showing that the will of men could triumph over ancestral fears, that order could reign over chaos.

This colonization was sometimes well accepted, and led to assimilation. One sign of this is the Nautes alter discovered in the 18th century in the foundation of Notre-Dame de Paris. This pagan altar was dedicated to the glory of Jupiter, but its four sides contain Roman gods together with Gaulish gods.

When the signs of Roman power were established on the island, life became more organized for a population which had been used to living, up until then, in thatched-roofed huts. This was nothing more than a miserable little town nestled behind the rough dikes that had been raised to protect them from floods. This is a naive image of tribal life, one of the many tribes that made up the turbulent nation of Gaul. Its people lived from fishing, and their geographical location slowly led them to become masters of river boating. The wealth of the future city of Paris was born in the waters of the Seine.

As the island quickly became overcrowded, the colonizers planned the development of a real city, in the same way their Roman cities were set up. The Romans were great builders, and they drew up plans for a city on the left bank of the Seine, and sealed its future.

Paris at night is full of contrasts. It goes from the wild neon lights of its lively neighborhoods to the almost provincial image that is found at its heart, at the very source of the city.

Rome in Paris

The Latin Quarter

The Cluny Museum, with its medieval collection, was the dream of Alexandre du Sommerard, who had purchased the Hôtel des abbés de Cluny: he wanted to recreate a place which would highlight the very spirit of the Middle Ages, and present its artistic treasures. The medieval period is here in harmony with the vestiges of the ancient world.

The Arènes de Lutece (Lutetia Arenas) are neither as large nor as majestic as those found in Nimes or Arles, in the south of France. But they add a space of silence and greenery to the heart of crowded Paris, with the small public garden that has been built there.

While it was swampy to the north of the île de la Cité, the land on the southern side of Paris was much better for building a city. The Bièvre flowed through this area, in a calm valley, and the montagne Sainte-Geneviève had gentle slopes where villas with terraces and closed gardens could be built. This was Rome along the Seine.

There were roads leading to Orléans, Sens, Autun and Burgundy. At the spot where this network of roads left Lutetia to connect it with the far provinces, there was a main road which was a local version of the Via Appia, which headed straight away from the Cité to the far horizon, through the vineyards.

This would be the main road in a quarter which would be developed much later, after the Middle Ages would see it become the student quarter. This is what would become the Latin Quarter.

Rome was very present, with its monuments, landmarks and arenas, just slightly off the main road which ran along the Palais des Thermes de Julien. On the sides of the montagne Sainte-Geneviève (what is now the rue Soufflot) there was a building that little is known about, but is speculated to have been a temple

dedicated to Jupiter. It did not survive the first attacks of the invaders who came to Paris, or the considerable expansion of Christianity, which would change the face of Paris.

You would need to look toward the Butte Montmartre to find another temple, this one dedicated to Mercury. And it was from here that the roads that led to the northern provinces left the city.

There are few traces left of Roman Paris, and what remains was so completely integrated in the development of the city that it is embedded in the very texture of this urban landscape. The Thermes (Roman baths), with their magnificent halls, became a part of the hôtel des abbés de Cluny, which would become, after many changes, and thanks to the collections acquired by Alexandre du Sommerard, the Cluny Museum (the National Museum of the Middle Ages). This museum bears witness to the exceptional medieval heritage of Paris.

Roman Paris progressively changed into the medieval Paris that François Villon, a child of this quarter, sang about, and the home of the rebellious students who would later hold their meetings in this neighborhood.

Page 17:
Through its recumbent effigies, all of France's history can be seen in the stone, marble and memorial fervor of the Saint-Denis Basilica. The tomb of Louis XII, who died in 1515, and of Anne de Bretagne, who died in 1514, was sculpted in Tours and is ascribed to the Italien sculptor Jean Juste. The addicula rises above the base in the shape of a catafalque, which presents the recumbent effigies, and on the upper platform, statues of the two deceased praying. Under the arches, the Twelve Apostles can be seen, and at the four corners are the four cardinal virtues.

Paths of Piety

The Saint-Denis Basilica

The Saint-Denis Basilica, just north of Paris, is the necropolis where the kings of France are buried. This site of pilgrimage is marked by a long history that makes it one of the most peculiar and attractive monuments in the Parisian area, although it is actually in its suburbs.

Now that Paris was Romanied, the message of Christ would slip into it. Secretly.

Denis came, perhaps, from Athens (but this has not been proven), via Rome, the city where Nero sent Peter and Paul to prison. He was accompanied by two companions, Rusticus and Eleutherus, who would share martyrdom with him, along with a few other future saints who had important roles in the History of this area (Saint Quentin in the Vermandois, Saint Crépin and Saint Crépinien in Soissons, Saint Valère and Saint Taurin who preached in Évreux, Senlis, Pontoise, Reims and Montmorency). Denis and his two companions preached in a remote place (near what is now the rue Denfert-Rochereau) but angered the representatives of the Roman administration. Denis was jailed in the Glaucia prison (on what is now the quai aux Fleurs) until one day in 287, when he was taken from the prison, thrown in chains, and led along the paved Roman way (what is now the rue Saint-Martin and the rue Montmartre). The procession reached the top of the hill taking what would become the rue des Martyrs. Eleutherus and Rusticus refused to renounce their faith and were beheaded (there are streets bearing their names near this spot as a reminder). As for Saint-Denis, he miraculously picked up his head in his own hands and carried it to a place where a compassionate woman came to his help. Denis gave her his head, and fell to the ground. She buried him there.

It was King Dagobert who, much later, gave the Basilica its later purpose as a royal burial site when he decided to place his own tomb there. Since then, most French kings have been buried inside this church, which was rebuilt by Suger at the beginning of the twelfth century. This is the Basilique Saint-Denis, which has close ties with French history.

Another legend that tells of the relationship between Lutetia and Christianity is that of Sainte Geneviève. So much mystery surrounds her that her life and family were invented for the legend. But her place in History was made when, as Attila and the Huns were approaching Paris, in the middle of the 5th century, she managed to assuage the fear of the Parisian population who wanted to flee the city. This courage gave her the role of protector, as posterity has proven (there is a statue of her

The Panthéon, this massive and imposing edifice, was built on the site of one of the first religious buildings in Paris, which had been originally ordered by Clovis and his wife, and dedicated to Sainte Geneviève. It was later replaced by the newer building built by Soufflot, after the wish made by the Parisian population for a church if Louis XV managed to live through a serious illness. This later became the Panthéon, with its reference to the ancient monument, during the French Revolution, which wanted a building to be used as a necropolis to honor its most worthy citizens.

In this wide view, the Panthéon can be seen to be in perfect harmony with the tall buildings in the quarter near the place de l'Italie. A symphony of domes and roofs creates wonderful rhythms in the sky.

on the pont de la Tournelle) and there is a sanctuary dedicated to her on the top of the mountain which bears her name.

The progressive implantation of the quickly growing catholic Church, with its wealth which linked it to monarchical power, would mark out the city of Paris with a multitude of buildings designed for different uses (convents, basilicas, chapels, parish churches, and even a cathedral) that have only left a vague memory behind, because the actual traces have been erased by the many changes in the urban fabric.

On the île de la Cité alone, where baron Haussmann applied his principles of urban rehabilitation more than in the rest of the city, there were almost two dozen small churches, including the one dedicated to Saint-Denis-de-la-Chartre where the Glaucia prison had been. Today this church is gone, and on its site, a flower market now stands.

The surface of Paris has been furrowed by time, overturned by the destructive energy of men, and this texture, which is both rich and sparkling, tells both of violence and pleasure, of faith and mercantilism.

While Clovis and Clotilda were responsible for the birth of the Sainte-Geneviève abbey (today the Panthéon) by creating the Abbaye des Saints-Apôtres, Childebert is responsible for the creation of Notre-Dame when he moved the Episcopal see to the île de la Cité from where it had been up until then, in a church of the Faubourg Saint-Marcel.

Wealthy abbeys were built within a sphere that covers far more than just the city of that time, with Saint-Victor in the southeast (the jardin des Plantes), Saint-Martin to the north (Musée des Arts et métiers), Saint-Germain-des-Prés to the south, Saint-Antoine to the east as well as the Temple, a city within the city, to the northeast.

Paths of Pilgrims

Saint-Julien, Saint-Séverin and the others

In 1646, Ann of Austria laid the first stone of the Saint-Sulpice church, which was considered too small even before it was completed. Le Vau took over its construction, making it larger. Only the choir, the side aisles and the transept were completed in 1678. The nave was finally finished in 1736. Then Servandoni, who had been entrusted with designing the square in front of the church, which was to include a semi-circular parvis and a group of similarly designed houses, built the church's facade with its two floors of porticoes. Maclaurin and Chalgrin designed the uneven towers. It was in the Saints-Anges chapel (the first to the right after entering the church) that Delacroix painted two of his masterpieces, including Jacob Wrestling with the Angel, *from 1853 to 1861.*

As much as roads are made by and for merchants, they are also made by the timeworn footprints of pilgrims. In close proximity to merchants' routes, pilgrims also need places to stop and rest, pray, and get bed and board. A geography of faith was established over time in Paris, as the city received travelers coming from the north to the south, and its religious congregations lived according to the rhythm of visits and receptions for those who, carrying their possessions over their shoulders, did not hesitate to travel the many miles to honor the saints that were their protectors.

Oddly enough, it was during one of the most terrible reigns, soaked in fratricidal blood (from the death of Clovis to Clotaire), that Paris saw the construction of some of its religious buildings which were most closely linked with the growth of Catholic faith. New parishes were formed on both banks of the Seine: Saint-Julien, Saint-Séverin, Saint-Merri, Saint-Étienne, Saint-Marcel, Saint-Gervais and Saint-Lazare. Each one of these churches was built around a piously donated relic, or to celebrate miraculous actions that helped the fearful population, bringing comfort to their souls.

Amidst the turmoil of political history, in spite of external aggressions, an architectural program was developed. Buildings were built, often thanks to the generosity of rich donors and the piety of the masses who found reassurance in their faith while they lived a life of cruelty, deception, difficulty and danger. The church, which was becoming more powerful, and more involved in the practical aspects of city life, admirably orchestrated the collective enthusiasm of the people of Paris. A multitude of bell towers, naves and pulpits were being added to the urban landscape, and they gave rhythm to day-to-day life. With time, Paris would become the city of a thousand bell towers, as can be seen in Fouquet's wonderful paintings, and in the illuminations and earliest woodcuts and etchings that show the Parisian skyline. This was the Paris of faith, which was living its most intense years and its most exciting moments.

This is the third version of the Saint-Germain-l'Auxerrois church (the first one was built in the 7th century). It was built to honor the memory of the bishop of Auxerre, "Saint Geneviève's spiritual father". This church is of differing styles, and was often modified. It was the church of the royal parish. Isabelle, the daughter of Isabeau de Bavière and Charles VI, was baptized there, as was Marie-Isabelle, the daughter of Charles IX and Elisabeth of Austria, and, much later, the daughter of Louis XVI, Madame Royale. François I often visited this church when he was at the Louvre, as did Henri III and Louis XIV, before he left for Versailles. As the church of the Louvre parish, Saint-Germain-l'Auxerrois was "the Saint-Denis of Genius and Talent", where many artists and writers who lived in the Louvre were buried, such as Jodelle, Malherbe, Stella, Sarrazin, Le Vau, Coypel, Israel Silvestre, Coysevox, Nicolas Coustou, Robert de Cotte, Restout, Boucher, Chardin, Jacques-Ange Gabriel. It was the bells of Saint-Germain-l'Auxerrois that sent the signal that began the massacre on Saint Bartholomew's day, August 23, 1572. A mass is held there each year on Ash Wednesday "for all the artists who will die in the coming year", according to the legacy of the painter Adolphe Willette.
To the right, illuminated scenes from the Bible.

Page 22:
This is the third church built on this site, dedicated to Saint Gervais, and construction was begun in 1494 but did not proceed very quickly. While its nave is in the flamboyant Gothic style, its facade, built by Salomon de Brosse under the reign of Louis XIII, is in the "Jesuit" style. The small chapels off the northern side aisles are at the location of a very old cemetery. Philippe de Champaigne is buried in the Communion Chapel. Madame de Sévigné was married in this church in 1644. The Couperin family had the charge of this church's organs for a very long time.

Page 23:
Saint-Germain-des-Prés was an abbey founded by Childebert I, the son of Clovis, to house the tunic of Saint Vincent and the True Cross of Salomon. This is where its original name, Saint-Vincent and Sainte-Croix, came from. Childebert died shortly after the church was consecrated. He was buried there, as were the Merovingians afterwards. The church was given the name Saint-Germain when the bishop of Paris, who died in 576, was buried theres. The church was sacked several times by the Vikings, and rebuilt in successive stages up until the 12th century, with monastery buildings surrounding it. There are only a few vestiges of these structures remaining, which can be seen in some of the buildings along the rue de l'Abbaye. It later became a parish church in 1791, was alienated by the Revolution, and was once again used for church services as of 1803. It underwent a great deal of renovation under Baltard, who commissioned frescoes from Hippolyte Flandrin. Among the famous people buried in this church are Descartes and Boileau, who had first been buried with the members of his family in the cemetery of the Sainte-Chapelle, where his father worked as a legal clerk.

THE STOMACH OF PARIS

The "Les Halles" quarter

The medieval landscape of Paris was full of towers and bell towers, but today there are only a few rare vestiges of these remaining. The tour Saint-Jacques carries with it a powerful legend and an occult power which fascinated esotericists and poets, including Gérard de Nerval, who committed suicide at the foot of the tower, on the rue de la Vielle-Lanterne, which no longer exists. André Breton saw in this tower a sign of vigilance: "In Paris the tottering tour Saint-Jacques / Stands like a sunflower / Its facade sometimes clashes with the Seine / And its shadow slides imperceptibly among the tugboats".

From 1851 to 1857, Baltard built "pavilions" on the site of the central market, Les Halles, which had been created under Louis VI, the Fat. This king had decreed that they be installed in the area called Les Champeaux, from which he received tax revenues. Napoléon III inaugurated these new buildings in 1857. The bold new design, using iron girders to create clear, airy roofs, which allowed a great deal of light to come through, were innovations that would later be imitated by many. This style was copied by many other French cities for their own covered markets.

It was Louis VI, the Fat, who decreed in 1136 that the covered market in Paris should be definitively moved to a field called les Champeaux, which was a bit away from the city itself, but along several often used roads. It was necessary to bring merchants together, for safety reasons, and to ensure that the Parisian population had sufficient supplies of food and manufactured goods. Completing the work begun by his predecessor, Philip II Augustus, had buildings built in 1183, "so drapers and weavers could sell their wares protected from thieves and bad weather", which would be called les Halles (the covered markets), and this name was given to the entire quarter. The huge amount of business done there attracted a shady group of people, along with "strumpets", who brought sacrilege to land hallowed by the presence of the cimetière des Innocents. This quarter remained somewhat seedy for centuries.

One of the appeals of Paris is the terraces of its many cafés. They give people a chance to take a rest, in a much-appreciated friendly environment. The renovation of old buildings in the Les Halles neighborhood enshrines them in historical surroundings.

The rue Aubry-le-Boucher is a very old street that dates back to medieval Paris; it was created in 1225. At number 18 is a church dedicated to Saint Josse and Saint Fiacre, the patron saints of gardeners.

There is a dense network of streets which connects the Carré des Halles with the rest of the quarter around it. Drapes came along the rue Saint-Denis from Senlis and Rouen, wheat came from the northern plains along the rue de la Ferronnerie, and fresh fish came along the rue des Poissonniers (Fishmonger's Street; this is how it got its name). As the covered market became organized, this helped fuel growth for the quarter and its surrounding area. Each reign made its own improvements, demolishing hôtels owned by lords and creating new streets. Even today, in this quarter, traces remain of its activity, which covered every aspect of retail trade. There are many trade guilds present here: drapers, haberdashers, grocers, hosiers, furriers and goldsmiths. A major reorganization was carried out under the reign of Henri II. The structures that were determined at this time were used as a framework for the huge renovation carried out by Baltard, under the orders of Napoléon III. The architectural boldness of using "iron, iron, nothing but iron" made it possible to have huge picture windows, and this would remain a model for future works of this type.

The boulevard de Sébastopol was created by Haussmann. Before he redesigned the city, the Les Halles quarter went on toward the neighboring Marais, in a maze of small streets which still retain something of their medieval aspect. The Saint-Jacques-de-la-Boucherie church was the parish church of this quarter, and its name was taken from the neighboring Grande Boucherie (Large Slaughterhouse). Legend says that it was partly financed by Nicolas Flamel. This church was used as a meeting place for guilds of butchers, hatters, hosiers, and gunsmiths, which made it an integral part of the social life of the neighborhood. The church was destroyed during the Revolution, but its bell tower remains. It became an almost magical marker, endowed with mysterious powers, in the poetic space reserved for Paris (from Gérard de Nerval to André Breton). And it was at the summit of this bell tower, which is decorated by statues showing the four symbols of the Evangelists: an Angel, a Lion, an Ox and an Eagle, together with a statue of Saint James himself, that Pascal is said to have carried out experiments on falling bodies.

The astonishing crowds who came through this area, inspired many authors to write lively descriptions about it. It was Émile Zola with his novel *The Stomach of Paris*, who managed to write the most powerful descriptions of this quarter, while including a vivid account of social life of the time. With his novel *The Stomach of Paris*.

LE PRÉ-AUX-CLERCS

Student life, the Sorbonne

There are a few angry verses that criticize the Saint-Michel fountain, written when it was built in 1860: "This dreadful monument / Shows no talent, no taste / The devil is worthless / Saint Michel does not deserve the devil." It has, however, become part of the romantic landscape of Paris. A laid-back and fun-loving crowd can often be seen gathering at its feet. This is the heart of the students' quarter, the beginning of the boulevard Saint-Michel that was praised by Francis Carco. The boulevard of bohemia and poetry incarnated by Verlaine, and the friendly poets of the school of the "Fantaisistes".

The Sorbonne has been progressively extended, and now occupies a number of religious and school buildings, including the collège de Cluny. It was in the chapel of this school that Jacques-Louis David painted Le Sacre de Napoléon (The Coronation of Napoléon). Girardon's masterpiece, a sumptuous mausoleum, commissioned for Richelieu's tomb, can be seen in the chapel of the Sorbonne.

The pré-aux-clercs (Clerks' Meadow) is a locality at the end of the huge Reine Margot garden (where the École des Beaux-Arts is located) which was once called "Little Geneva", because the Huguenots had used it for their secret meetings. It was part of the University and students ruled this area, hence its name. Originally, before the University was officially established around the Sorbonne, it was made up of a number of different colleges whose chancellors were also officials in different religious congregations. Between the city wall built by Philip Augustus and what is now the place de l'Odéon, there were many different colleges, with names such as the collège d'Autun, collège de Boissy, collège de Tours, collège de Bourgogne, collège des Cordeliers and collège d'Harcourt. These were often very small institutions funded by the bishops of the cities whose names they bore. The rue des Écoles (School Street) is a reminder of the early activities that occurred in this quarter. Some of these establishments would go on to develop and stand out because of the quality of their scholarship. These are the lycées (roughly, middle schools or high schools) Saint-Louis, Louis-le-Grand and Henri IV, whose creation spans several centuries. These schools were breeding grounds for talent, and were the starting points for many political or cultural careers.

The small collège de la Petite Sorbonne, whose name comes from its founder, Robert de Sorbon (1271), was one of the most remarkable centers of student life. It developed an extraordinary reputation, and it became a fine illustration of university life when many large

The rue de Bièvre takes its name from the Bièvre river which was diverted from its original course to bring water to the gardens of Saint-Victor (where the Jardin des Plantes is now located). This street, which was created in 1224, follows a path which became a sewer and which ran into the Seine. Dante is said to have lived here in 1295, and to have written part of his Divine Comedy. Other famous inhabitants of this street are the poet Crebillon (1674-1762), and Restif de la Bretonne who lived here in 1776. This was the period when he would wander at night on the Ile Saint-Louis and carve the names of his mistresses on the parapets along the banks of the Seine.

buildings were built around it, which are even now at the heart of the University of Paris. Its benefactor, Cardinal Richelieu, was buried in a tomb designed by Girardon in the chapel of the Sorbonne, itself designed by Lemercier, to commemorate his invaluable assistance.

The 17th century saw a reorganization of student life, by reinforcing its links with the exceptional richness of religious life, whose great names of the time were Saint François de Sales, Saint Vincent de Paul, Sainte Jeanne de Chantal (the grandmother of Madame de Sévigné), cardinal de Bérulle, Bossuet and Massillon. Great architectural endeavors were begun at this time, such as the Val-de-Grâce complex (commissioned by Marie de Médicis) and the creation of the college des Quatre-Nations (by Mazarin) which has since become the Institut, where the Académie Française meets.

Mazarin, just like his mentor and inspiration Richelieu, created this college whose name clearly indicates its purpose: it was to receive sixty students who had been granted scholarships, selected from the noble families of the four nations that had recently been reunited with France, or which depended on its administration (Pignerol, Alsace, Flandres-Artois-Hainaut and Luxembourg, as well as Roussillon, Conflans and Sardaigne). It was built by Le Vau, who was then working on the Louvre, at the site of the old hôtel de Nesle, whose tower was still standing, and which had become legendary since Alexandre Dumas used it as the site where the princesses of Philippe le Bel's family carried out their debauchery.

This school was quite a distance from the Sorbonne, but since it was part of the Saint-Germain-des-Prés quarter, it managed to avoid the excitement of the boulevard Saint-Michel. This was the main center of student and literary life from the end of the 19th century to the beginning of the 20th century, according to Francis Carco, who wrote some of the most valuable texts about this exciting time. Carco was, along with Paul Jean Toulet, one of the figureheads of the group of poets known as the "*fantaisistes*", and during this time they would cross paths with Verlaine and Rimbaud. Literature was also at home in the dark little shop run by young Charles Péguy just alongside the powerful Sorbonne. With his literary magazine, *Les Cahiers de la Quinzaine*, he forged links between literature and politics. Politics would use the "boul'mich", as the boulevard Saint-Michel was called familiarly, as a stage for some of its "street happenings". In May 1968, it became the stage for many exulting revolutionary actions.

The café des Deux-Magots, along with the café de Flore, was one of the centers of cultural life in the years when the Saint-Germain-des-Prés quarter was popular. It was founded in 1885, in the place of a curio shop, and from this shop the two Chinese grotesque porcelain figures (magots) that gave it its name remain. It was the stage for Alfred Jarry's practical jokes, Léon-Paul Fargue's late night revelling, (he also frequented the brasserie Lipp), and served for a while as a meeting place for the Surrealists before they left to go to other locations. Many other famous people also spent time here, including Apollinaire and Remy de Gourmont before the First World War, Derain, Picasso, James Joyce, Paulhan and Malraux in the Roaring Twenties. A literary prize (the Prix des Deux Magots) was created in 1933 as a result of this creative excitement. Raymond Queneau was the first to receive this prize.

Page 35:
The seat of the different Académies (Académie Française, Académie des Beaux-Arts, etc.), the Institut was originally the Collège des Quatre-Nations. Along both sides of the chapel, designed by Le Vau, were series of small shops in arcades where prints, books, paintings and furniture were sold. The father of the painter Chardin ran a cabinetmakers shop here. This building was used as a prison during the Revolution, and it housed, among others, David, doctor Guillotin, and Madame de Touzel of Marie-Antoinette's retinue. David also had a studio here.

Cafés and restaurants with many different facades, and many different styles, line the streets of Paris for the pleasures of pedestrians. Paris still has its gourmets like Grimod de la Reynière, or Gault and Millau.

The Café de Flore dates back to the Second Empire. Its name comes from a small statue of Flora that used to be just above its main entrance. The Action Française (the French Action, an influential right wing anti-republican group in France in the early 20th century) was created on the upper floor of this café. Apollinaire would often come to this café, and together with André Salmon he created Les Soirées de Paris (Paris Evenings), which attracted the young poets who later became the group known as the Surrealists. It was the peaceful provincial atmosphere of this café that attracted Simone de Beauvoir and Jean-Paul Sartre during the Occupation. They came here to have a warm place to write. After the Liberation, the café was extremely popular because of the "bande à Prévert" (the Prévert group) and a number of other artists and poets who would later become legendary like Artaud, Giacometti, Adamov, Audiberti, Jean Genet, Jacques Laurent, Boris Vian, Mouloudji, Serge Reggiani, Juliette Greco and the young "Lettristes".

There are many nostalgic old-fashioned restaurants along the old streets of the Latin Quarter near Saint-Germain-des-Prés, such as Le Petit Zinc (The Small Bar). Traditional social values based on the art of eating well are perpetuated here.

A small bistro open to the street. These meeting places are proving grounds for popular thinking, spontaneous opinions, and are the site of picturesque ironic vocabulary, places where anything can happen, the kind of meetings that André Breton called "illuminating". The Surrealists were known to drink a great deal of coffee during their meetings.

The passage du Commerce, in the Odéon quarter, was at the heart of revolutionary Paris. Docteur Guillotin did experiments with the instrument of death that bears his name, and Marat had a printing press here. Danton lived at the end of this passage. It runs from the boulevard Saint-Germain to the rue Saint-André-des-Arts, and goes along the rear of the restaurant Le Procope.

While the place du Tertre, in Montmartre, is the "official" place for painters who sell their wares on the street, many other impromptu exhibits can be seen along the sidewalks of Paris. In the area around the Centre Georges Pompidou, along the fences of the Saint-Germain-des-Prés square, and wherever artists think they will find their customers.

From One Palace to Another

The Palais de Justice, the hôtel Saint-Pol, the Louvre, the Tuileries

The Sainte-Chapelle church was designed by Pierre de Montreuil, at the request of Saint Louis, to house the crown of thorns which had been purchased from Venitian merchants who had bought it from Baudoin II, the last French Emperor of Constantinople. A piece of the True Cross was later bought directly from him. The audacious architecture of the building has a huge, high space and a vast amount of light, and its shape is similar to that of a reliquary. It was the scene of many prestigious religious celebrations, as well as the coronation of Isabeau de Bavière in 1389. During the Revolution, it became a warehouse for archives, and was later sold. It was fully restored from 1840 to 1857 by Duban, Lassus and then Viollet-le-Duc.

In 1246, 615 square meters of stained glass windows were installed in the Sainte-Chapelle. Out of the original 1,134 scenes, inspired by the Old Testament, 720 of them have survived, in spite of serious damage during a fire in 1630, and the use of the church as a warehouse for archives during the Revolution.

Royalty and royal authority took up residence in a palace on the île de la Cité, at the site of what had previously been the seat of the Roman administration. The Merovingians ruled the city and later the Carolingians; but these were traveling rulers, and the former were later known as the *rois fainéants* (do-nothing kings). After the Vikings attacked and sacked the city, a Capetian, Robert the Pious (996-1031), undertook new construction, and this was to continue, with the exception of the tip of the island which was saved for an area with gardens and orchards. Each king added his own touch to the edifice that was the île de la Cité. It was Louis IX (Saint Louis) who had the largest addition built on the island, the Sainte-Chapelle, designed to house the relics of Christ, including his crown of thorns. Philippe le Bel adorned it with his gallery, and Charles V added the tour de l'Horloge (Clock Tower) which, together with the bell tower of Saint-Germain-l'Auxerrois, rang out to set in motion the Saint-Bartholomew's day massacre in 1572, during which thousands of Protestants were killed in Paris. Many Parisian monuments, including the most sumptuous ones, are stained with the blood of History.

The future Charles V left his residence in 1357 and moved into the hôtel Saint-Pol (or Saint-Paul), on the right bank. This was actually a group of houses connected by

"That one building, whose construction was overseen by kings, emperors and even republics in the course of centuries, can offer such unity, such simple greatness; that such a building is in no way an architectural mosaic; this is truly magnificent", exclaimed Leon Bopp in Paris. The Louvre developed along with the succession of reigns that lived together with it. From the Renaissance (right) to its extensions at the end of the 19th century, it is a precious setting for the art that it contains and presents so well.

The construction of the Pyramid, at the key spot where visitors enter the Louvre Museum, is the work of the Chinese-American architect Ioeh Ming Pei. Its pure strict shapes are the completion of the geometric outline of the different wings that make up the Louvre Palace. The same spirit is behind the design of the inverted pyramid in the Carrousel shopping center.

galleries, crisscrossed by paved courtyards, gardens, arbors, and even a small zoo and other places for amusement. Because of this, it was also called the hôtel Saint-Pol of "frolics". It was protected by the nearby Bastille. But nothing of this palace remains, with the exception of some streets whose names serve as a reminder: rue Charles-V, rue des Lions, rue du Petit-Musc, rue de la Cerisaie, rue de Beautreillis.

In 1407, the Crown purchased the hôtel des Tournelles which had belonged to the uncle and brother of Charles V. Its name comes from the wall of its huge garden which is lined with little towers. It was located in an area which is now delimited by the place des Vosges, the rue des Tournelles, the rue Saint-Gilles, the rue de Turenne and the rue Saint-Antoine. Like the hôtel Saint-Pol, it was made up of a series of private houses, chapels, wash rooms, and outbuildings connected by wooden galleries, and this compound surrounded two parks, six gardens and even some small woods. The rue du Parc-Royal (Royal Park street) reminds us of this. Charles VII, Louis XI, Charles VIII and Louis XII, all lived here, and Louis XII died here as well. François I was more attracted by the Loire valley châteaux and Fontainebleau, but his son Henri II spent his last days here, after the accident he suffered at a tournament in July 1559. His grief-stricken widow, Catherine de Médicis, left this accursed palace and too

k refuge in the Tuileries, the palace she had built next to the Louvre. It was at this spot, which was then the limit of the city of Paris, surrounded by protective walls, that there was a palace called the Louvre. While this was not the king's usual residence, it was used by his administration. Charles V had his famous library here.

This defensive structure was turned into a castle when Philip Augustus was building the new city walls of Paris (1190). Since there was still fear of an invasion coming from the Seine, as the Vikings had done a few centuries earlier, the king wanted to reinforce his defenses on this side of the city. The castle built there was a true medieval castle, with a keep, crenellated walls, moats, and deep dungeons. You can still see the strong solid foundations in the current Louvre, since archeologists have restored them.

Charles V later added a second wall and improved the living conditions of the fortress. He designed this marvelous palace, topped with gilded and painted weather vanes, and oriflammes, which can be seen in the miniature paintings in the *The Very Rich Hours of the Duc de Berry*, by the Limbourg brothers. This fairy-tale

The Cour Napoléon in the Louvre. The razing of this area gave Haussmann a chance to "learn about demolitions". Between the Louvre's north and south wings was a maze of small streets and houses, old hôtels and even a church (Saint-Louis-du-Louvre) which ruined the view that the designers of the palace desired. Balzac took walks here, and spoke of a "dark deserted block of houses where the inhabitants were probably ghosts, because you hardly ever see anyone... Already buried by the raising of the place du Carrousel, these houses are shrouded in the eternal shadows cast by the high galleries of the Louvre, darkened on this side by the north wind. The shadows, the silence, the chilled air, the cavernous depth of the ground all contribute to make these houses like crypts, living tombs...".

Rue des Orties, rue du Doyenné (the street of Nerval's friends), rue Frometeau, rue Saint-Nicaise, rue Saint-Thomas-du-Louvre, where the famous Hôtel de Rambouillet was built in the 17th century, the lively meeting-place for the Précieuses, with the blue room where Arthénice (Catherine de Vivone) received the intellectuals of the time. When this space was cleared, Haussmann designed two consecutive squares, with a mediocre decoration of trees and plants, and a monumental statue of Lafayette, sculpted by the American Paul W. Bartlett, a student of Frémiet. An energetic statue by Paul Landowsky was added to the second square: The Sons of Cain. This all disappeared with the recent construction of the pyramid, which opened the space of these squares.

*Page 50:
The transformation of the Louvre to a museum was a very long process, which was conditioned by an evolution of the concepts of museology. At first, the museum was accumulative, and its goal was a quantitative inventory. It later became more selective, and started taking into account the way its objects were presented. This led to environments specifically adapted for these objects, which had to be developed within an architecture that was not at all designed for this purpose. Many wonderful marriages of works and their surroundings resulted, which greatly contribute to the appreciation of the objects being presented.*

While the Louvre was once a palace where protocol ruled, as a museum it is now a space for discovering art, which is often done in a playful manner.

A palace before being a museum, the Louvre has conserved some of its most splendid decorations, including this ceiling, in the Greek room, which bears witness to the luxury of day to day Court life.

castle would progressively become the palace of all the French kings, and as each one took up residence there, they made their own contribution, enlarging it. As it got bigger, the fortress disappeared. It was slowly transformed from its rugged medieval shape to that which we now know, a building of grace, acquiring the personality of each of the reigns that it lived through, in a magnificence equal to its role as the seat of power.

Louis XIV, who had fled Paris during the Fronde, had decided to move the seat of power to Versailles, leaving the Louvre, that he had enlarged (the Colonnade was designed by Claude Perrault to complete it), to artists and the different parts of his administration. The building would not be reused for its royal function again until Napoléon. By then it was already connected to the Tuileries by the Grande Galerie, that runs along the Seine.

The history of the Louvre is intertwined with that of the Tuileries' palace. When Catherine de Médicis moved in to the Tuileries, she was fleeing death. She had a great love of luxury, and knew that wealth had a political dimension, and participated in giving credibility to power. Catherine called on the leading architects of her time to create a palace, whose name comes from the tile factories *(tuileries)* that had been located on the same spot.

Philibert Delorme, who was succeeded by Jean Bullant in this huge undertaking, constructed a large building which would go through many changes over the centuries, and which was connected to the Palais du Louvre by the Grande Galerie, during the reign of Henri IV.

This palace was a huge, powerful and complex status symbol. Its unity comes from the intelligence of those who undertook to expand it, adding state-rooms, while the royal apartments were in its oldest section, along the Seine. After the winds of Revolution swept through the country in 1789, the Tuileries' palace was taken over by Napoléon and his court, and became the monarchs' palace until Napoléon III, who added the final touch by bringing the building up to date with the fashions of the time, just before it was burned down under the Commune in 1871. The only remaining example of this time is the extravagantly luxurious drawing room, which can still be seen in the Louvre. Before becoming a museum, according to the wishes of the revolutionary Convention, the Louvre and the Tuileries palace were the theater of official life, the mirror of monarchic splendor. This splendor underlies every chapter of the history of Paris.

A Dramatic View

The Champs-Élysées

The Parisian street is the theater of large popular sporting events, such as the arrival of the Tour de France or the Paris Marathon.

After Le Nôtre designed the Tuileries garden, he cut a straight alley through the adjoining woods, which was a tip of the forest of Rouvray, to extend the view. The part closest to the future place de la Concorde was paved; this is the Grand Cours, which received its name to distinguish it from the Cours-la-Reine that runs along the Seine. At the time, this was a disreputable and even dangerous area before the first hôtels were built there. The first series of hôtels built along the Faubourg Saint-Honoré had its gardens here. These were sumptuous hôtels that were gradually torn down to make room for rental buildings. Those that remain were completely changed to take on their new functions (banks, office buildings). The Champs-Élysées quickly became a myth, incarnating a certain Parisian luxury with restaurants such as Ledoyen and le Fouquet's, and Gay Paris, with the Lido and today the Queens. The part of the Champs-Élysées that runs along the Grand Palais and the Petit Palais is greener, and contains theaters (Marigny, Ambassadeurs) and the buildings by Hittorf which were the stage for the young Marcel Proust's childhood, and whose charm he described in Within a Budding Grove. *As a lavish entry, just off the Champs Élysées, one can see the* Chevaux de Marly *(Marly Horses) by Coustou, (these are copies, the originals are in the Louvre) which recall the two groups by Coysevox which stand on either side of the entry to the Tuileries garden.*

The facade of the Tuileries palace, a brilliant mixture of the different contributions of the various architects who worked on it, closes off the huge complex of the Louvre palace that it is connected to by the Grande Galerie that runs along the Seine.

A new Paris was begun here, with an admirable view designed to look westward toward the spectacle of the setting sun.

The design of the Tuileries Garden, which was also refined over a period of several centuries during several reigns, progressively found its unity thanks to the genius of Le Nôtre, who would later use his talent for the Parc de Versailles, just as the king was beginning to prefer Versailles to the Louvre-Tuileries complex.

In 1757, the aldermen of Paris decided to create a square just outside the garden, in honor of Louis XV. This became the place de la Concorde after having been, during the Revolution, one of the main stages for executions, and the site where many of the period's most important people were beheaded (Louis XVI, Marie-Antoinette, Charlotte Corday, Danton, Robespierre).

The sinister guillotine stood not far from the place where you can now see the Obelisk of Luxor, which was brought back from Egypt under the reign of Louis-Philippe, and which marked the beginnings of "Egyptomania" which has increased ever since. There are attractive naiads spouting water in the two fountains around it.

There are eight monuments around the square, which incarnate French cities, and which are raised high on pedestals, acting as sentries.

The two beautiful hôtels designed by the architect Gabriel close off this square on the side of the growing

La Défense completes the view that was begun in the courtyard of the Louvre. It is a hymn to modern architecture, and its playful additions are the work of some of today's greatest artists, from Nicolas Schöffer to Calder.

Chance juxtapositions, giving strange encounters, can sometimes underscore the age and richness of the history of Paris.

Saint-Honoré quarter. However, to the west, there were still the thick woods of what remained of the old Rouvray forest (the Bois de Boulogne). There was a wooded view, much like what Le Nôtre would later create at Versailles, and which gave Paris one of its nicest views.

As if by magic, the disappearance of the Palais des Tuileries (burned by the Communards in 1871), and the enhancement of the Arc de Triomphe in the Cour du Carrousel, which at that time was the "city side" gate, fit this view into the crucible of the oldest part of the Louvre. There was now a view from this, the very heart of French official life, that stretched as far as the magnificent gate of the Arc de Triomphe at the place de l'Étoile. And today, this horizon stretches even further to the bold skyline of La Défense and its Grande Arche, which was designed precisely to be in line with this view.

Now that Paris was open to the west, magnificent sunsets could be seen from its center. The most imaginative people, or the most megalomaniac, even imagined extending this triumphal view to the sea.

This view only highlighted the dynamic of a city set on continuing its growth toward the setting sun and following the course of its river, taking its path of fantasy, following the gently and voluptuous curves that would carry the incomparable charms of its nonchalant banks to its distant suburbs.

The organizers of monarchical life, who wanted to create a worthy setting, soon recognized this impetus. The ascent of the Champs-Élysées is a sort of modern version of the path to heaven evoked by mythology that this avenue, The Elysian Fields, refers to. The 19th century saw the creation of some of its most ostentatious, luxurious homes, so appreciated by the nouveau riche and their mistresses. Only a few buildings remain which bear witness to this period, such as the hôtel de la Païva, which was the home of a

The Tuileries garden was designed at the same time as the Tuileries palace was built, under the orders of Catherine de Médicis. It has constantly evolved since then. At first, a collection of plants which mirrored the palace in the Renaissance style, it was completely redesigned by Le Nôtre, and enlarged to take its place in a more global vision of a city of Paris which was growing toward the west. It was Charles Perrault, the author of Tales, who managed to obtain permission for the public to have access to this garden as long as they were "neither beggars nor servants nor soldiers". The painter Poussin lived in one of the houses in the garden, after the king had called him to work for the Court. During the Revolution, Robespierre organized the Festival of the Supreme Being in the garden, and the heavy circular marble benches that were installed for this can still be seen there. The cenotaph erected in honor of Jean-Jacques Rousseau, when his ashes were transferred from Ermenonville to the Panthéon, can be seen on the large pool at the entrance to the garden.

The fountains of the place de la Concorde are part of a large-scale development plan directed by Hittorf from 1836 to 1840. Statues representing French cities (the ones of Lille and Strasbourg are by Pradier) were placed at the eight corner houses, which had been imagined by Gabriel in 1754, and there are rostral columns, framed by street lamps and balustrades, as well as two fountains inspired by those in Saint Peter's square in Rome. The southern fountain is at the place where Louis XVI was guillotined on January 21, 1793. It is dedicated to the divinities of the sea, while the northern fountain (by the rue Royale) is dedicated to the river divinities. In between them is the Obelisk of Luxor that was brought to France under the reign of Louis-Philippe and installed there in 1831.

schemer who flaunted her splendor by giving herself a cultural hallmark which could excuse her excesses. This is where the flower of the world of art and literature of the "fin de siècle" gathered around the Goncourt brothers, in an atmosphere of voluptuous luxury created by Carrier-Belleuse, a precursor and mentor of Rodin.

Halfway along the Champs-Élysées, toward the place de l'Étoile, is a tree-lined spot where the young Proust developed his sensitivity "*Within the Budding Grove*", where the triumphalism of the 1900 World Exhibition left as a witness to this time two palaces standing face to face, and whose names placed them in a hierarchy of scale, the Petit Palais (small palace) and the Grand Palais (large palace). They are both representative of the "fin de siècle" style, with their excessive ornamentation, their generous curves, their charming embellishments and their highly feminized shapes.

Swamps and Gossip

The Marais

There are some very old houses which remain in the Marais quarter. This part of Paris has managed to withstand the ravages of time and the large urbanization projects that slowly leveled the city. Today, these final remainders of such a rich past attract the greed of real estate promoters and are the delight of those strollers looking for vestiges of the past. Although it came late, the awareness of the value of these houses was strong enough to save what could still be saved. The rebirth of the Marais quarter is proof of this.

For a long time this quarter, the Marais (which means marsh), was flood land, and unfit for building. Here and there, in areas that had been spared by flooding, religious congregations settled. As the marshes were progressively dried out, parishes were founded and churches built: Saint-Martin-des-Champs, Saint-Nicolas-des-Champs and Notre-Dame-des-Blancs-Manteaux. At the time that the hôtel Saint-Pol was the residence of the king, prominent members of the Court, and other lords, built houses in the neighborhood, on both sides of the rue Saint-Antoine. The flirty Isabeau de Bavière, who was being wooed by the brother of Charles VI, the wealthy Louis d'Orléans, had a house on the rue Barbette. Louis' assassin, his cousin Jean sans Peur (John the Fearless), the duc de Bourgogne, whose hôtel was at the western end of the Marais (what is currently 20 rue Étienne-Marcel) had a strong tower built to protect himself, since he felt threatened by the turmoil which opposed the rival de Bourgogne and d'Armagnac families. Medieval art is well represented in many aspects of the Marais, such as the enclosure around the Templar domain and the Célestins convent, the different churches (Saint-Jean-en-Grève, Saint-Gervais, Sainte-Catherine du Val des Écoliers and Saint-Paul) and the different mansions, the hôtel de Sens and the hôtel de Clisson (which has since become a part of the hôtel de Rohan-Soubise).

While the Middle Ages saw the construction of housing in this quarter, it was during the Renaissance that development increased substantially. Many of the buildings of that period have since disappeared, but the hôtel Carnavalet and the hôtel d'Angoulême are fine examples of the magnificence of this period. Many

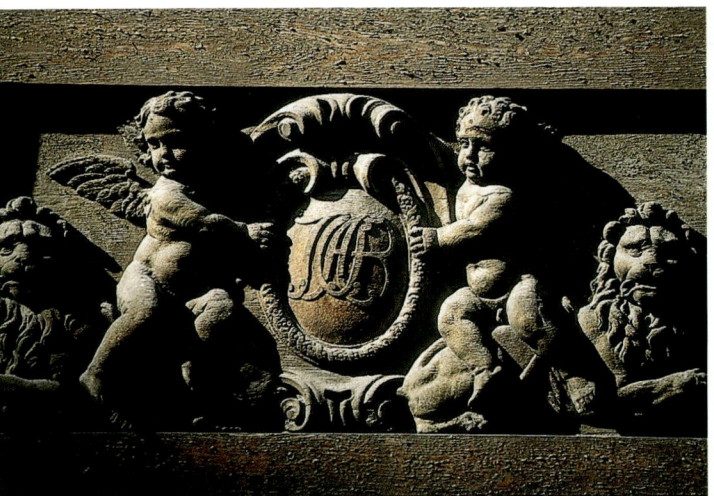

A carving on the Hôtel Amelot de Bisseuil. Located at 47 rue Vieille-du-Temple, the Hôtel Amelot de Bisseuil is also called the "Hôtel des Ambassadeurs de Hollande" (the Dutch Ambassadors' hôtel), and this name comes from the fact that it was once rented to the Dutch Ambassadors' chaplain. It belonged to several people, including Henriette de Coulanges, the sister of Marie de Coulanges, the mother of the future Madame de Sévigné, and mother-in-law of Madame du Deffand, whose salon was famous in the 18th century. Pierre Augustin Caron de Beaumarchais rented it, and used it as a depot for arms that were to be sent to the American rebels. He completed his play The Marriage of Figaro while living at this address. Mademoiselle Necker, the future Madame de Staël was baptized in the chapel of this hôtel.

Below, a carving from the Hôtel Carnavalet, and another from the Hôtel du Grand Veneur.

The Hôtel de Sens is one of the finest examples of medieval architecture in Paris. This hôtel was the residence of the archbishop of Sens (which is where it gets its name from) who was a superior of the bishop of Paris. In 1605, Queen Margot, the daughter of Catherine de Médicis, who was separated from Henri IV after having married him for political reasons, came to live here. She was an "easy" woman whose lovemaking was noisy, and she left this hôtel after the death of her lover, the son of a carpenter, that she had compromised herself with. She then moved into the hôtel that had been built specifically for her at the Pré-aux-Clercs (at the location of the École des Beaux-Arts, the School of Fine Arts) and scraps of this building still remain on the rue de Seine (from number 2 to 10).

Page 62:
The Hôtel de Lamoignon is now occupied by the Bibliothèque Historique de la Ville de Paris (Historic Library of the City of Paris). This was originally a simple plot of land belonging to the Sainte-Catherine priory, and was used as a dueling field before the Hôtel Robert-de-Beauvais was built here in 1558. Diane de France, the duchess of Angoulême (an illegitimate child of Henri II, later legitimized), purchased it in 1584, demolished it, and had the building we now see there built. This became an important cultural center. Her heir, Charles de Valois (another royal illegitimate child: the son that her half-brother Charles IX had with Marie Touchet), completed its construction. He was very old, and married a very young girl who lived in this hôtel until 1713. She rented part of it to the president of the Paris Parlement, Lamoignon, and his heir purchased it in 1688, which explains the name that it has worn ever since. The hôtel was divided, and in the 19th century, it contained shops and a bourgeois apartment. The author Alphonse Daudet, who had recently married, moved in here in 1867. It was at this address that he wrote Fromont the Younger and Risler the Elder, whose setting is inspired by the Marais.

splendid houses were built during the 17th century, and it was these buildings that gave this quarter its character, its style and an art de vivre, which placed this quarter under the aegis of the *Précieuses*, who, despite Molière's assertion, were not always ridiculous. This quarter started becoming important when the place Royale (the current place des Vosges) was created, which was a vast operation ordered by king Henri IV himself, and whose harmonious layout heralded a style of architecture whose splendor would be discrete. This was the true birth of the Marais as an aristocratic quarter. It was soon covered with hôtels built for the kingdom's leading families (Montmorency, Guénégaud, Rohan, d'Albret and Châtillon).

The rue Saint-Antoine, which ran along the Bastille, and which started with a ceremonial gate at the foot of this dark fortress, was the main southern thoroughfare of this Paris of wit and fashion. Along the sides of this road were the hôtel de Mayenne, the hôtel de Sully and the churches, l'Église de la Visitation-Sainte-Marie and l'Église Saint-Paul-Saint-Louis.

To the north was the splendor of the rue des Francs-Bourgeois; a splendor which has, in some places, faded with the passing of time. This street ends at the hôtel de Rohan and the hôtel Soubise, now the location of the National Archives.

Several streets cross the Marais from north to south (rue des Archives, rue du Temple, rue Vieille-du-Temple) which connect the center of the capital to this Templar domain. Nothing remains of this domain, with the exception of the square built at the location of the garden that separated the famous tower where the royal family was imprisoned from the fine hôtel du Prieur, which was the home of several royal princes or favorites with purely honorific titles, who succeeded the great medieval figures who had led the Knights Templar to their fortune. There was a gradual shift from a religious and military function to a situation of pure privilege that was sometimes promoted, even justified, by their patronage. Was it not here, in conditions not fitting for his genius, that the young Mozart was able to play as a child prodigy as his father dragged him from court to court across Europe?

The spirit of the 17th century developed thanks to key figures such as the future Madame de Maintenon, who was then only the wife of the witty Scarron, and who held a salon at the corner of the rue Saint-Claude and the rue de Turenne; Mademoiselle de Scudéry, heiress to Madame de Rambouillet, who received the high society at the rue de Beauce, and who was the same person who flocked to the antechamber of the beautiful Ninon de Lenclos in the rue des Tournelles. And of course Madame de Sévigné, in her hôtel (today the museum Carnavalet), who held writing workshops and carried on one of the most delightful correspondences ever imagined with her daughter.

When the court moved to Versailles under the order of Louis XIV, the neighborhood emptied, and fell into the decay that has only recently been overcome. In the 19th century, the Marais was a neighborhood of small craftsmen who had their shops and workshops in the courtyards of the aristocratic hôtels that had been left empty, and which became greatyl disfigured. Some of these hôtels, which had been abandoned for a long time, were progressively and carefully restored. The first of these, and one of the best examples of the rebirth of this quarter, is the hôtel de Sully (62 rue Saint-Antoine) which was built for its namesake, and which later became the Caisse Nationale des Monuments Historiques et des Sites (Ancient Monuments and Historic Buildings Commission). Others include the hôtel d'Albret (31 rue des Francs-Bourgeois) now the Center of the Cultural Affairs Department of the City of Paris; the hôtel Guénégaud (60 rue des Archives), which is now the Musée de la Chasse and de la Nature (the Museum of Hunting and Nature); the hôtel Libéral Bruant (1 rue de la Perle) which is now the Musée de la Serrurerie Bricard (the Bricard Lock Museum); the hôtel d'Aumont (7 rue de Jouy); the hôtel Salé which was dramatically and efficiently restored to become the Musée Picasso.

It was in the admirable hôtel de Lamoignon (which is now the Bibliothèque Historique de la Ville de Paris, the Historic Library of the city of Paris), which was split into apartments, where Alphonse Daudet wrote most of his works. His work, written in an abandoned shell of architectural splendor, was sometimes a mirror of his strangely popular environment.

This hôtel, built according to plans made by a descendant of Doctor du Cerceau was sold in 1634 to Maximilien de Béthune, the duc de Sully, former minister of Henri IV, who gave the hôtel its name. He was a man at the end of his career, but lavished with wealth and honors, and he moved into this hôtel and adorned it in luxury. At the end of the garden, he built the Petit Sully (the Little Sully) which opens directly onto the place des Vosges (number 7). It was in the courtyard of this hotel that Rohan Chabot insulted the young Voltaire. This episode deeply marked him, and lead him to be imprisoned in the nearby Bastille for one year. After a period of decay in the 19th century, and a judicious restoration, it became the center of the Caisse Nationale des Monuments Historiques (Ancient Monument and Historic Buildings Commission).

Grotesque masks and knockers in the Marais quarter.

Squares and Celebrations

From one square to another

Memories of the most famous residents of the past cross paths at the place des Vosges, as children's laughter rings through the central square. This square is a space where there are magical meetings between the past and a vibrant present.

Before the Louvre was finished, and connected to the Tuileries by Napoléon III, what is now the place du Carrousel was a group of houses and old hôtels which made up a quarter which did not have a very good reputation. Romantic bohemians lived there, in the famous impasse du Doyenné. Théophile Gautier was one of the leading figures and Gérard de Nerval left souvenirs of this quarter in his Little Castles of Bohemia.

The organization and enlargement of a city depend on its network of roads. Streets cross the city but also cross each other. When a square is born, it is often the meeting place for several streets that run along it before heading out to conquer the constantly receding horizon.

Some squares are designed artificially (place des Vosges, place Vendôme or place Saint-Sulpice) as the setting for monuments, or to highlight certain facades. Many squares are just stopping points along a path or breaks in a journey, which make it possible to diversify the path being followed, to change it, or to head in new directions.

An exception to this rule is the place du Carrousel, which, for a long time, served as the main courtyard of the Tuileries palace, and its Arc de Triomphe became the entrance. It was inaugurated with great pomp, and its name comes from the fact that it was used for a lavish equestrian tournament whose star was the young Louis XIV. Prancing on a spirited horse, he gave the image, as time would show, of an audacious man who was not afraid of showing himself off.

While some squares are merely for display, others fit closely into the complexity of the city's network of roads, and influence their traffic. Squares like this are integral parts of the neighborhoods whose very nature they define. One such example is the place Victor-Hugo in the elegant 16th *arrondissement*. Created in 1826, and

The place du Trocadéro followed the original project of creating a place du Roi-de-Rome (King of Rome Square), which included a palace of the same name, that was replaced by the Palais de Chaillot. The name for this square comes from the Fort du Trocadéro, which had been removed during the Restoration by the French during the Spanish military campaign in 1825. At the center of the square is a tall statue of Maréchal Foch riding a horse, which is the work of Robert Wlérick and Raymond Martin (1951).

The place de Furstenberg was the road that had been opened in 1669 by cardinal Egon de Furstenberg to give access from the monastery of Saint-Germain-des-Prés to the rue Jacob. It was the courtyard used for the stables. It was here, at number 6, that the painter Delacroix lived his last years (1857-1863). His apartment has become a museum bearing his name.

then named the rond-point Charles X (the Charles X traffic circle), it owes its current name to the avenue which runs across it, which is an homage to Victor Hugo, who died at number 124 of this avenue in 1885.

Another square that can be seen in a more recently constructed neighborhood is the place du Trocadéro. This stands below the huge terraces of the same name, which provide one of the most extraordinary views of the capital with the Eiffel Tower and the Champ de Mars just across the Seine.

Nearby are two other squares (place de l'Alma and place d'Iéna) that border it at the two ends of a road which goes to the Musée d'Art Moderne de la Ville de Paris (the Paris Modern Art Museum) and the Palais Galliéra, whose name comes from the duchess of Galliéra who had this building built in the Italian Renaissance style in 1880. This building served different purposes before becoming the Musée de la Mode et du Costume (the Fashion and Costume Museum).

The place d'Iéna is a hub for many streets: the avenue d'Iéna, avenue du Président Wilson, avenue Pierre Ier-de-Serbie, rue Boissière, and rue de Longchamp. It leads to the Musée Guimet which has large collections of art from Asia and the Far East, and whose name is taken from the donor of most of its collections. It is also at the place de l'Alma that Courbet and Manet each had temporary buildings built to expose their works at times when their paintings were disapproved of by institutions and scorned by the public.

Another beautiful square is the place de la porte Dauphine, along the edge of the Bois de Boulogne, which was built by Alphand during the reign of Napoléon III. This is one of the most spectacular entrances to this wooded park, which was, in the 19th century, the showplace for socialites. This was immortalized by Constantin Guys who, according to Baudelaire, gave a heroic accent to the characters of the human comedy, cramped in their tight boots and narrow pants.

The place des Ternes, on the site where the barrière du Roule (the Roule gate) had been, serves to distribute traffic to this quarter where the Paris of the plaine Monceau ends, and the Étoile quarter begins. The center of this square holds a permanent flower market, with beautiful accents of the provinces.

There are two squares that stand out because of the charm they inherit from their daily use, and their daily visitors. The one called the place des Fêtes is far from the center of Paris in the working class quarter of

The Tuileries gardens were first a royal garden before becoming a popular space. The majesty of its layout is somewhat disturbed each year when a fairground is set up in the garden, and this huge Ferris wheel is one of the main attractions. While not everyone appreciates it, it adds its own special brightness to the dark night. Here, between the obelisk of the place de la Concorde and the Ferris wheel, is the clash of centuries.

Belleville. Its name comes from the celebrations (fêtes) which took place there when it was just one of those small quiet villages that surrounded Paris, before being swallowed up by the city in 1860 to become another neighborhood of the growing city.

Even older, the place d'Aligre was built in 1778 on land which had been part of the Saint-Antoine abbey. It is now the site of a picturesque market for food, clothes and bric-a-brac.

Picturesque is also the best word to describe the place du Tertre, which is the end of all the paths leading up the Butte Montmartre. One may start the ascension at the place Saint-Georges, at the heart of the Nouvelle Athènes quarter, then cross the place Adolphe-Max, where the rue de Calais, rue de Vintimille, rue de Bruxelles and rue de Douai meet. It was here, before the Revolution, that the Folie Bouëxière which Jacques Hillairet called "a real Petit-Trianon", referring to the small château built in the park around Versailles, presented small hidden streets, bowers, icehouses, refreshment stands and games. All that remains are the trees in the central square.

Going further on up the hill, you cross the place des Abbesses, after having strolled along small streets which follow the ancient paths from the time when this was the Montmartre abbey, whose entrance was on the square. Up a few steps from here is the quiet, unadorned place Émile-Goudeau, that was a very inspired place during the years that the Bateau Lavoir was the center of artistic activity in Montmartre. Reminders of this square can be found in the mocking *Poems* of Max Jacob, and in poems by André Salmon and Francis Carco who both went there often.

The left bank has been marked by the centuries that have gently flowed by, carrying with them the extensive development around the structures left behind by the gallo-roman city of Lutetia. These traces can be seen in the heart of the place de la Contrescarpe, which was only built recently, in 1852. This square is the result of a harmonization of local housing, which was so old that the famous Pomme de Pin cabaret (Pine Cone Cabaret) described by Rabelais, was located here. This cabaret had a close relationship with the Pléiade writers (Ronsard, Joachim du Bellay, Jodelle...). Almost a neighbor, the place de l'Estrapade was an important hub in the Middle Ages. Its name (which means strappado) comes from the terrible torture that was applied on this spot to recalcitrant soldiers. There is an excellent view of the dome of the Panthéon from here. If

The place Louis XV, inaugurated in 1757, was designed to highlight a statue of "Le Bien-Aimé", the Beloved King, which was commissioned by city aldermen from Bouchardon. It was octagonal and surrounded by a moat and balustrade, and highlighted by eight pedestals (which are still present). During the Revolution, this was the scene of much bloodletting when a guillotine was erected on this square. The north side of the place de la Concorde is bordered by two colossal hôtels by Gabriel. One, which is now the Navy headquarters, was designed to be the royal store. The other has become the Hôtel Crillon, named after the family who owned this hôtel starting in 1788.

In the 14th century, the place du Tertre was contiguous with the boundary wall of the Montmartre abbey. Trees were planted there in 1635, and a gallows was installed. It was used as a storage area for cannons in 1870, and the government's order to remove them from the square was at the origin of the first popular uprising that led to the Commune. Since it was "outside the walls", this part of Montmartre declared itself an independent community. A town hall was built (at number 3) which still has its traditional character. Now taken over by the terraces of the many cafés that surround it, and by painters exposing their works, the place du Tertre has developed a slightly stilted but picturesque atmosphere, where the idea of a certain type of easy-going Paris is seen.

Shakespeare and Company is one of the many bookstores in Paris which is also a reading room, carrying on a long tradition. It played an important role in the evolution of literature. This was the case for the bookstores owned by Adrienne Monnier and Sylvia Beach, on the rue de l'Odéon, in the 1930's, and the store owned by the poet Marcel Béalu "Le Pont Traversé" in the 1960s.

you go down along the montagne Sainte-Geneviève, you come across the place Saint-Michel, which was built in the middle of the 19th century and contains a fountain made by Davioud.

In the natural flow of traffic from Saint-Michel to Saint-Germain-des-Prés, the carrefour de l'Odéon (Odéon crossroads) is another consequence of baron Haussmann's urbanization, which led to the destruction of Danton's house. An imperious effigy of this eloquent speaker can now be seen there.

There is a beautiful view of the théâtre de l'Odéon from the end of the rue de l'Odéon. This street played an important role in the literary history of the 20th century, because it was here that Adrienne Monnier had her famous bookshop, Aux amis des livres, which was a meeting place for such writers as Gide, Valery Larbaud, Claudel, Reverdy, Léon-Paul Fargue, Aragon, Breton and Paul Valéry. Shakespeare and Company, the bookshop owned by the American Sylvia Beach, who first published James Joyce's Ulysses, was also on this street. The beautifully curved place de l'Odéon, along with the Café Voltaire, is also a landmark in literary history, where Alfred de Musset, Gambetta, Verlaine, Mallarmé, Paul Gauguin and Rodin were regular visitors over the years.

There is one very discreet square, that looks as if it were hidden by the buildings surrounding it: the place Furstenberg. It owes its uncommon shape and charm to the fact that it was once the main courtyard of the monastery, of which only one building remains along this square. Delacroix also had his studio here at the end of a small courtyard, that has the same charm it did in Delacroix's time.

While the route from the montagne Sainte-Geneviève to Saint-Germain-des-Prés is a road lined with literary and artistic history, the route from the Bastille to the place de la République has a very important social and symbolic function. It is here where, up until the time when Haussmann started his works, there were many little theaters. They gave their name to the nearby boulevard, which was then called the "boulevard du Crime", by allusion to the popular plays that were presented here. The creation of the grandiloquent monument by Léopold Morice, devoted to the triumphant Republic, helped name this huge square which surrounds the large statue: the place de la République. On the base of this statue, where onlookers gather during parades and demonstrations, are twelve bronze bas-reliefs which tell the story of the

Tightrope walkers used to do their acts on the Pont-Neuf, during the Saint-Germain fair. Today they are more often seen around large monuments, and always gather spontaneous crowds who throw coins to them to thank them for their efforts. They are part of the scenery of Paris, just like in novels by Victor Hugo.

The Hôtel de Ville, the Paris City Hall, at one of its more relaxed moments. This square is used for many popular events.

great moments of the French Revolution. This is a little known and picturesque sort of sculpted comic strip.

Another square in the center, in the oldest part of Paris, is the place de l'Hôtel de Ville, which, for a long time, was called the place de Grève (the Shore Square), because at that time it was just a plot of land running down to the Seine. The name of this square is now a commonly used word, grève (strike), because it was on this square that unemployed workers would gather.

At the same time as the merchants of Paris moved into what would become the Hôtel de Ville (city hall), the square became organized and became a key space in the daily life of the city. It was used for seasonal festivals as well as for torturing condemned prisoners. Depending on their rank, they were hung, drawn and quartered, axed or stabbed with swords (for gentlemen), or burned (for heretics and witches). This was an opportunity to gather, a pretext for unrest or

Let us follow the footsteps of Léon Bopp, author of Paris: "Along the rue Mouffetard, this nice working-class and even friendly street, there are many delightful stalls, and especially butchers' stalls where you can see small signs stuck into steaks and chops that say "I'm tender, buy me!..."."

dubious gatherings for a population of thrill-seekers. Many famous people were sacrificed to the public here including the brother-lovers of the princesses of Burgundy (part of the history of the Tour de Nesle), Ravaillac, Henri IV's assassin (1610), Damiens who had attacked Louis XV (1757), la Brinvilliers, the poisoner who had compromised Louis XIV's mistress, la Montespan (1676) as well as the accomplice of La Voisin (1680).

This square was also used, during the darkest days of the Revolution in 1789, as a sounding box for the passions of a people who were fickle and easily carried away by the desire for vandalism, and who saw Lamartine defend the French flag here during the 1848 Revolution.

The King's Honor

The place des Vosges, the place Dauphine, the hôtel des Invalides

*The place des Vosges.
To replace the Hôtel de Tournelle, where Henri II spent his last days after being wounded during the fatal tournament of 1559, a horse market was created. Henri IV decided to build an ambitious project there for a square where all of the houses surrounding it would have identical facades. A huge operation of real estate speculation mobilized society, and the leading families moved in. Among the well-known residents were the Coulanges family, whose daughter Marie married a Chantal. They were the parents of the future Marquise de Sévigné and lived at 1 bis. At number 11 lived Marion Delorme, a courtesan from the time of the Précieuses, while legend has it that the person who best represented the spirit of the times, Catherine de Vivone, marquise de Rambouillet (who was living in the hotel bearing her name), briefly lived at number 15, in 1618. Number 23 belonged to Marie-Charlotte de Balzac d'Entragues, the elder daughter of Marie Touchet, a former mistress of Charles IX and sister of Henriette d'Entragues, a mistress of Henri IV. There are many royal boudoir stories in these shadowy surroundings. The Hôtel Guémenée, number 6, was inhabited by Victor Hugo from 1830 to 1848. While living here, he wrote Lucretia Borgia, Marie Tudor, Ruy Blas, The Burgraves, Inner Voices, Light and Shadow, and The Last Day of a Condemned. Number 8 was the home of Théophile Gautier, from 1831 to 1834, who wrote Mademoiselle de Maupin while living here, and Alphonse Daudet later lived here.*

Victor Hugo said it simply: "It was Montgomery's spear thrust that created the place des Vosges", referring to the tournament where Henri II lost his life. The square was first a horse market, and the site of the famous duel of Henri III's mignons, and among others, the duel of the grandson of Henri de Guise (Coligny's assassin) and surprisingly Coligny's grandson, in a lover's quarrel. At stake was the favor of Madame de Montbazon and Madame de Longueville. Trees were not planted until 1783 and 1872, and a garden was created in 1866. In the center of this square was an equestrian statue of Louis XIII that was first made in bronze, then melted down during the Revolution when supplies were needed for the war, and later rebuilt in marble. This marble version was made by the 19th century sculptor Cortot.

As the center of power, the residence of the king, and the showcase of French culture, Paris has always lived according to the rhythm of the different reigns that have ruled it. The Bourbons (starting with Henri IV), more than the other dynasties which came before them, were sensitive to the prestige that could come from the splendor of the city, and took care to improve its appearance. Of the grandiose projects started by Henri IV (including a place de France which was north of the Marais quarter, on the side of the old Temple), the only reminders are the names of some of the streets in the neighborhood (rue de Bretagne, rue de Saintonge, rue de Picardie, rue de Normandie, rue du Poitou). The appearance of this neighborhood was changed considerably, but he did accomplish one last ambitious project, is the harmonious place des Vosges (then called the place Royale), which was built on land that had belonged to the Palais des Tournelles, abandoned by Catherine de Médicis after her husband, King Henri II, died accidentally.

To complete the construction of the Pont Neuf (the oldest bridge in Paris, in spite of its name, which means the New Bridge), which had been decided by Henri III, Henri IV also had the houses of the place Dauphine built. This area contained ruins of the ancient king's palace and garden, and the tip of the island ended in a sort of muddy shore where there were a few small wild islands, including the Ilot aux Juifs (the Jews Islet) where stakes were erected to burn the last Knights Templar. This is now called the square du Vert-Galant.

The medieval shape of the Conciergerie can be seen in this view along the river, highlighted by the Pont-Neuf. This large complex of buildings dates back to the 15th century. From this period the Tour Bombec, the Tour d'Argent and the Tour de César remain; this latter tower is the place where Fouquier-Tinville installed his offices during the creation of the Revolutionary Tribunal, and prison cells were built inside the old palace. These legends remain, greatly deformed by naive piety, marked by the memory of the famous victims who spent time there, especially Marie-Antoinette.

Construction of the place Dauphine required that land be filled in, and this was part of a theatrical desire of the king to show off, which could be seen by the equestrian statue of the king which was added to the tip of the island in 1614. This statue, destroyed during the Revolution, was replaced by an obelisk designed by Bélanger, and placed on a rocky area. With great romantic enthusiasm, it is described as "terrifying rocks where the waters would well-up and crash violently in fierce chaos, at the foot of the bridge, with elephants on either side…" This was just another project, like the public baths imagined by Guy de Gisors with imperious Roman facades.

But this was a unique location in Paris, both central and symbolic. The bridge was the stuff of wild dreams, and, for many years after its difficult construction, it would be crowded with strange comic characters. In the 18th century, there was a sort of art market on the place Dauphine where such painters as Boucher, Chardin, Lancret, and Nattier exposed their works. This tradition endured, and Goncourt is said to have purchased paintings there by his favorite 18th century painters, that he later helped bring back into style.

More than just an architectural signature in the city, Louis XIII's reign brought new energy, and this period saw the building of many new private homes, and the progressive enrichment of the Marais, which attracted the aristocracy who brought with them luxury and splendor. He oversaw the creation of a new city wall, which included the newly built quarters to the north and the east of the capital. Starting at the porte de la Conférence (between the Tuileries terrace and the Seine) it went to the porte Saint-Honoré (at the corner of rue Royale and rue Saint-Honoré), and followed what would later become the Grands Boulevards, punctuated by the porte Gaillon (at the corner of the rue du Quatre-Septembre and rue de la Michodière), porte Richelieu (the corner of the rue Richelieu and rue de la Bourse), porte Montmartre, porte de la Poissonnerie and porte Saint-Denis.

Louis XIV's reign saw large construction projects which put the finishing touches on the enlargement of the city, with the creation of the Hôtel Royal des Invalides, and the closing of the Louvre's Cour Carrée by the Colonnade, which was the work of doctor Claude Perrault, the brother of the author of the famous *Tales*.

Finally, there are two squares that helped contribute to the celebration of the king. One of them, the place des Victoires, was commissioned by a clever courtier, the

The hôtel des Invalides complex was designed by Libéral Bruant, and the church and its dome by Jules-Hardouin Mansart. These were built under Louis XIV's orders to house old soldiers who were invalids. This large uninhabited tract of land between the Faubourg Saint-Germain and the Gros Caillou was selected, and enough empty space was saved to highlight it, to give it the dignity corresponding to its function, and the majesty desired by the King who had commissioned it. With a huge esplanade in front of it, and built around several courtyards, and a garden, it follows the laws of geometry which were then popular, and the sobriety of its military role. It is inseparable from the space that it generates, and was used, along with the Champ de Mars, as a site for some of the World Exhibitions of the 19th century.

Page 85:
Place Dauphine was originally the king's garden, a plot of land to the western tip of the île de la Cité. When the Pont-Neuf was built, a handful of islets were connected (including the île aux Juifs where the Knights Templar were burned alive). The garden was urbanized under Henri IV. He ordered the first president of the Parliament, Achille de Harlay, to build the houses around what would become the place Dauphine in the shape of a triangle. The third side was destroyed when the Palais de Justice was enlarged. Many details on these buildings have been changed but a great deal of the original unity of the square is still visible. Manon Philipon, the future Madame Roland, the famous Revolutionary, lived in number 37 and later number 28 (41 quai de l'Horloge) at the time of her wedding in 1780. Ludovic Halévy, a key figure in the cultural life of the late 19th century, and a friend of Degas, died in 1908 at number 26.

The genius of Libéral Bruant can be seen in the development of a 210 meter long facade decorated by grotesque masks, helmets and flaming urns according to the spirit of the times. An elegant slightly curved forecourt is the entrance to the monumental courtyard where the church can be seen, which is used for large ceremonies. It is framed by statues of Mars and Minerva sculpted by Coustou. In front of this is the garden surrounded by a dry moat, containing cannons, including some captured by Napoléon in Vienna.

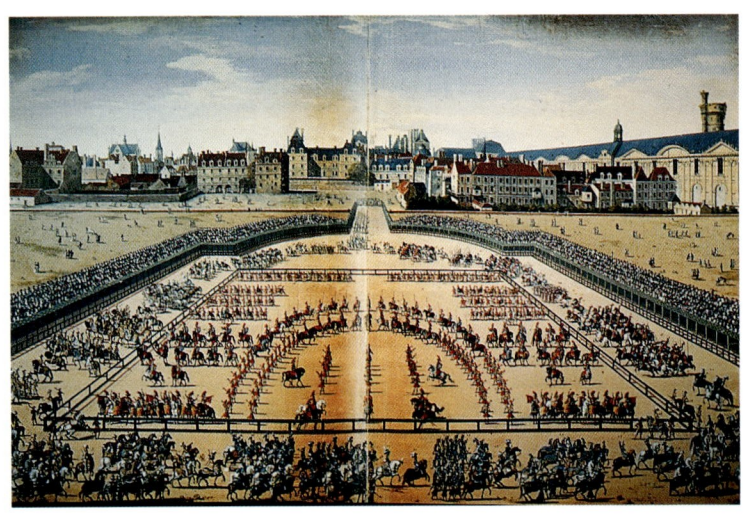

The Tuileries during the reign of Louis XIV. Louis XIV is seen here parading during a carrousel for the inauguration of this new space opened in Paris. The square, place du Caroussel, kept this name.

In the foreground, the Tuileries; in the background, the île de la Cité and the left bank surrounded by Philippe Augustus' city wall. Etching by François Hoiamis.

duc de la Feuillade. He was able to purchase enough land for this, and entrusted the development of the square to Mansart. Five streets met here: the rue Croix-des-Petits-Champs, rue de la Vrillère, rue de la Feuillade, rue des Fossés-Montmartre (today the rue d'Aboukir) and the rue du Petit-Reposoir (today the rue Vide-Gousset).

The place Vendôme was built on the instigation of the king. Louvois pushed the king to commission it, and this turned out to be an excellent opportunity for speculators, in spite of its very strict specifications which imposed a style of construction that would guarantee architectural unity (this was also the case for what is now the place des Vosges). This square was supposed to be built around an equestrian statue, in imitation of the place des Victoires, and for a while the possibility of connecting them together by a triumphant way was considered. Just like many urban projects, this one suffered from a lack of funds and took a long time to complete, and after many changes finally ended up as a homage to the glory of Napoléon.

It was purely out of indulgence for his soldiers that Louis XIV created the Hôtel des Invalides, in a quarter that was still undeveloped. He later decided to urbanize this part of Paris which was far from its center. The creation of the Observatory, at the edge of the seedy Saint-Michel quarter, was also due to a desire to concentrate some key activities in Paris which would reinforce its prestige, without encroaching on the political activities which were handled in Versailles. Colbert's always energetic activities energized the industries that would celebrate the greatness of the throne. It was he who selected the banks of the Bièvre river, the peaceful waterway which ran from the Poterne des Peupliers near la Glacière (icehouse), for the building of the manufacture des Gobelins (the Gobelins Tapestry works) where many of the Sun King's greatest realizations and mythological references were woven into tapestries.

The reigns of Louis XV and Louis XVI did not see such ambitious projects, and then the Revolution came, bringing a new chapter whose themes were utopias and vandalism. This chapter turned out to be dark and bloody.

Princely Whims

The Palais-Royal, the Palais de Luxembourg and the large hôtels.

Amidst the hustle and bustle of Paris, the Palais-Royal is a haven of peace.

Page 89:
This was supposed to have been called the place des Conquêtes (the Conquest Square) and later became the place Louis-le-Grand. Under the Revolution it was named the place des Piques, before finally taking its current name, the place Vendôme. It was designed by Jules-Hardouin Mansart and Boffrand. The column was built in 1810, replacing the statue of Louis XIV that had been designed by Girardon and which had been destroyed August 12, 1792, a hundred years after being built. This column is an imitation of Trajan's column in Rome, and at its top is a statue of Napoléon as Julius Caesar, designed by Chaudet and which was knocked over during the Commune (under Courbet's instigation). The statue by Augustin Dumont is inspired by this. A long series of bronze bas-reliefs surround the column and run 116 meters. They present the epic history of Napoléon's conquests.

Colette, looking from the windows of her apartment, wrote her memories on blue paper, and Jean Cocteau, her neighbor, distilled his sadness saying: "and the Palais-Royal emptied by Thermidor / its silence haunted by bluish lights / going coming in the shadows, between the two theaters..." In the romantic period, Charles Nodier came here to converse about letters with some of the poets of his circle and said "You will never see this small pool again in the garden of the Palais-Royal, the pool where Louis XIV fell in as a child, and which would make you think. It is strange to imagine what the France of our time would be like, if the young Louis XIV had drowned in a pool of the Palais-Royal." The history of France is sometimes born in woods and gardens.

When the king was in his palace at the Louvre, the princes who make up his court gathered attentively around him. To obtain his favors and advantages, they needed to be by his side. Louis XIV carried this principle to its extreme limits within the unity of the Versailles château where many noblemen, who owned large estates in the provinces and hôtels in Paris, accepted to live in attics to "pay their court". Each key figure of this frivolous, ruthlessly ambitious society, whose fate depended on the favors that the king would grant them, would do their best to reconstruct, within the limits of their personal fortune, the rules and customs, the principles and the rights of the Court.

Very near the Louvre, Cardinal Richelieu ordered the construction of a palace which, during his lifetime, was known as the Cardinal's palace, and when, on his deathbed, the cardinal gave the palace to the crown, it became known as the Palais Royal (Royal Palace). This is an admirable construction, and it has been renovated and enlarged by its successive owners, who include the Orléans family, when Louis XIV gave it to his brother the duke d'Orléans. This is where he grew up, and it was a center of power during the regency when Philippe d'Orléans took over after the death of Louis XIV and before Louis XV was old enough to rule. Later, an opera was built there, and a theater, and the Comédie Française moved in when it was reconstituted.

Page 94:
In the university quarter, the jardin du Luxembourg is a center for Parisian cultural life. It has inspired many of the writers who were regular visitors. André Gide, who lived nearby, came here to converse every day. He recalls this in The Counterfeiters.

Page 95:
The reading room designed by Labrouste in the Bibliothèque Nationale, on the rue de Richelieu. How many dreams, how many discoveries have been made among the pages of the books read under the light of the green lamps turned on early every afternoon. This is the main laboratory for literature in Paris.

The Pol Bury fountain at the Palais-Royal is part of a huge program designed to place contemporary art into the city. Works were commissioned from some of the leading contemporary artists who are developing the newest trends in art; Pol Bury, a proponent of "synethism", plays with movement, slowness, and geometry in his relationships with water. The calm modernity of this mirrored sculpture fits well in the atmosphere of this space.

The Palais du Luxembourg is also closely linked to court life. Marie de Médecis wanted to build her own palace modeled on the Palazzo Pitti in Florence where she had grown up. It was built in 1615 by Salomon de Brosse, close to the Petit Luxembourg, whose name came from the owner who had sold it to the queen. This name has remained ever since.

Rubens was commissioned by Marie de Médecis to make a series of large paintings to decorate the interior of the palace, paintings that can now be seen in the Louvre museum. Gaston d'Orléans inherited this palace, and after him, the Grande Mademoiselle became owner. History has left its trace here. It was a prison during the Revolution, a center of power during the Directoire and today houses the French Senate.

Along the rue du Faubourg Saint-Honoré, a street lined with many luxurious hôtels that bear witness to its popularity when it was still countryside, and some rich people came here to build their homes, stands the Hôtel d'Évreux, hidden behind high walls that once belonged to the marquise de Pompadour. She had this park enlarged and, in spite of regulations against it, added a sort of semicircle which encroached on the Champs-Élysées. This is now the Élysée palace, the residence of the French president. Over time it was owned by many people, including the financier Beaujon and the duchesse de Bourbon-Condé, the mother of the duc d'Enghien, who was shot by Napoléon. During the Revolution, the garden became a playful area where the lower classes would frolic in a jolly atmosphere. Murat owned it for a while, thanks to his brother-in-law Napoléon. But its role changed along with the unpredictable events of history, and many owners would live here until Napoléon III, who planned and carried out his coup d'état of December 2, 1851 in this hôtel.

Many of the palaces and hôtels that were built over the centuries by prominent figures in government have disappeared, or their functions have been changed so much that they no longer resemble the original buildings.

The current Palais des Archives is a remarkable example of this. It is an agglomerate of various houses which were connected, and makes up a sort of anthology of centuries which have accumulated in one area; lives, fates, famous people and fortunes, who were symbolically linked by this complex which is called the Archives.

The hôtel de Clisson (60 rue des Francs-Bourgeois) owes its name to the commander of the French army under Charles V who moved in here in 1372. The wife of François de Lorraine, the duc de Guise, moved here in 1553 giving his name to the building. It was greatly enlarged, and its history was closely linked to the dark hours of the wars of religion and the Saint-Bartholomew day massacre. Later belonging to Anne de Rohan, the wife of François de Rohan (in 1697), it was totally renovated, and the palace which today bears her name was built. Another Rohan, her brother-in-law, had built a mansion nearby, and a garden (now open to the public) was created to connect the two buildings. The architect Boffrand oversaw this work until 1745, and, because of different inheritances, the mansion was passed on to the famous Soubise, who had been nicknamed "the friend of the king's heart" because of his good fortune at the Court of Louis XV. It was finally inhabited by Cardinal de Rohan, whose naivete led him to be involved in the terrible story of the queen's necklace which heralded the French Revolution. The mansion was confiscated by the queen, who decided that it would be used to conserve the national archives. It has been used for this purpose ever since.

The Bibliothèque Nationale is another result of the Revolution, that decided to use Mazarin's palace for its location. Mazarin, who was part of the inner circle of Queen Anne of Austria when she was living with the young Louis XIV in the Palais Royal, had a beautiful hôtel

built (at 8 rue des Petits Champs) where he housed his large personal collection of art. To hold all of these works, he had Mansart build a two-storey gallery parallel to the rue Vivienne, which is still present and which now bears his name.

At his death, his collections went to the Crown, but the hôtel, divided up by his family, had several owners before finally belonging to Louis XV who, in 1724, decided to place the "King's Library" created by Charles V there. Major renovations were progressively made in the different neighboring hôtels, and they were then connected and unified by the building designed by Robert de Cotte (at the end of the main courtyard of the current library). During the Revolution, plans were made for a huge reading room designed by Boullée, which was never built. Labrouste later built a reading room, which is still there today.

After the popularity of the Marais quarter, under the reigns of Henri IV and Louis XIII, the Faubourg Saint-Germain (which today includes the rue de Varenne, rue de l'Université, rue de Babylone, and rue de Grenelle) became the preferred quarter of the aristocracy, creating a lifestyle, a clan mentality, and an idea of class which would go beyond the turmoil of the French Revolution to be reborn in the 19th century in a more constricted way.

While this aristocracy lost an important part of its political power, it lost nothing of its splendor and prestige for a bourgeoisie that wanted to rise to that level. The nouveaux riches created their own quarter of hôtels (private mansions), which competed with their splendor and showed off their wealth gained in stock market speculation, around the parc Monceau, in a quarter that had been designed by Baron Haussmann under Napoléon III.

19th century society was ruled by a constant series of relationships made by family alliances, and marriages of convenience, which brought together the great names and the young fortunes of this time. This is the society where Marcel Proust found the characters of his huge literary saga *Remembrance of Things Past*. This title shows well that between these two quarters there was a whole segment of social life that tried to impose permanence on their vision of the world, but this art de vivre disappeared totally after the painful experience of the First World War.

Brotherhoods and Watermen

The Hôtel de Ville

The esplanade of the Hôtel de Ville is a place for entertainment, relaxation and meetings. More than just a simple view or an open space to highlight a monument, it is a landmark in the life of Parisians. The Hôtel de Ville is, by definition, the communal house.

Saint Louis, the great organizer, created the first municipal institution in Paris, which allowed the bourgeoisie to elect their representatives. At their head was the provost of merchants, and a symbol, the famous ship of the Nautes, which would later become the city's crest, along with the motto "Fluctuat nec mergitur" (She is buffeted by the waves but does not sink). They needed a place to hold their meetings and assemblies, a building that would represent them with the dignity they deserved.

After trying a few different locations, they finally settled on the place de Grève, in the "*maison aux piliers*" (pillared house) before a specific building was built for them, a building which would grow through the years. It was destroyed by the Commune and rebuilt almost identically, with a great deal of ornamentation, by artists who were popular at the end of the 19th century (1883). The current building is a fine example of architecture and decorative art from the "fin de siècle".

Just like the Louvre, this other symbol of power, the Hôtel de Ville (the city hall) is a building that evolved slowly and took on the marks of many different styles before blending them into an exemplary unity. This building was later burned down under the Commune. But its growth meant more space was needed, and this was detrimental to the other buildings that occupied the land around it. Just as the Louvre led to the destruction

As the center of the city's administrative life, the Hôtel de Ville is also used for popular festivities which punctuate the daily life of its citizens. Here, in a tradition that dates back to medieval guilds, is the annual café waiters' race.

Some of the great moments in the history of France took place with the Hôtel de Ville as its stage. As a living symbol of Republican mythology, it is draped in blue, white and red to highlight its permanent presence.

Today's Hôtel de Ville was rebuilt after having been burned down during the Commune. Its architecture is inspired by the Renaissance, and the architects (Ballu and Deperthes) expanded it and cleared out the area around it. Sculptures for the square were designed by the Lalanes who created works that play with plants and water.

of houses and even religious buildings that surrounded it, the Hôtel de Ville led to the razing of its surrounding buildings. It has become the flamboyant and theatrical building we now know, in its current site along the avenue Victoria. But power often needs subterfuges for its credibility...

The architecture used for official buildings is never innocent, and their styles, which reflect the tastes of the period they belong to, do not obey time-worn recipes, that would be acceptable at any time under any regime. The facade of an official palace bears witness to the type and quality of power that resides within it. Its interior decoration, which is a perfect anthology of the pompous "pompier" style of painting that was popular in the 19th century, corresponds to a society which is satisfied by what it owns and has every intention of making these assets bear fruit. This was the temple of a new ideology where communal ideals brought back an old medieval idea, with the respect given to guilds, and lessons in civic responsibility. The people's house is also its museum. It has remained that way.

The Taking of the Bastille

Paris during the French Revolution

Among the many historians who wrote of Paris, Hofbauer was the one who best presented the climate of the city, thanks to his many detailed illustrations, which were reconstitutions in the taste of 19th century dioramas.

When the Bastille, which gave this square its name, occupied its southern section (there are paving stones that show the position of the fortress), the moat that surrounded it was connected to the Seine by an advancing glacis. The city gate (the porte Saint-Antoine) was built in 1585 and then included in the gate built by Blondel (the architect of the porte Saint-Denis) which was built in 1671. Statues by Jean Goujon were next to it. It was torn down in 1778. After its demolition under the Revolution, the square was briefly a site used for popular festivities. In 1833, the column was built, in memory of the Trois Glorieuses of 1830. A crypt beneath the column contains the bodies of the 504 victims of this uprising, together with mummies that Bonaparte brought back from his campaign in Egypt, which had been destined for the Louvre Museum, but which had decomposed. The tunnel of the Saint-Martin canal also passes beneath this column, before widening and flowing into the Arsenal basin.

The Bastille fortress, which was the result of a large program of defensive structures added to the city wall built in Paris during the reign of Charles V, was actually nothing more than the porte Saint-Antoine, a sort of reflection on the eastern side of Paris of what the Louvre was toward the west side. Medieval Paris had developed between these two imposing buildings. The Bastille was a strong squat rectangle, with eight towers (whose shape can be seen by the paving stones visible in the current place de la Bastille).

The towers were connected by a wall that was more than three meters thick and their tops were terraces with an exceptional view of the Saint-Antoine quarter that was growing on either side of a road first called the chaussée de Chelles. Its history is directly linked to the internal squabbling of the nobility during the Fronde. This quarter, which had a turbulent history, was where artists and furniture makers lived and worked, and according to the contemporary chroniclers of the French Revolution, "the crater from which revolutionary lava would most often flow". It was here that popular processions would start before crashing against the sides of the Tuileries palace like violent waves as the royalty was slowly dying.

The Bastille, which had become a jail where people who troubled public order or the comfort of the leading families were arbitrarily imprisoned, and which was one of the many dungeons where the famous Marquis de Sade was held prisoner, was symbolically attacked by the population on July 14, 1789, the date of the birth of an entirely new France which would become republican.

Freed from this cumbersome evil prison, this area did not quickly find a new purpose. People danced on the site of the demolished fortress, and a Fountain of Regeneration, something that the revolutionary regime greatly appreciated, was briefly built there, to mimic religious services while highlighting civil virtues. For a while, there was even a thought of building a statue of

The spirit of the Bastille is seen in this figure of Liberty flying in the air and breaking off its irons and casting light around it, a four meter tall gilded bronze statue by the sculptor Augustin Dumont. It is at the top of the column which took the place of a planned monumental fountain in the shape of an elephant, that Victor Hugo speaks about at length in Les Misérables, *and which is used as a refuge by Gavroche.*

an elephant, but this never saw the day. It is this elephant that Victor Hugo speaks of lyrically, as the dwelling of Gavroche, his sad heroic hero in *Les Misérables*.

It was after 1830, to celebrate the Trois Glorieuses (three days in July 1830 which ended the Restoration), that the Bastille again became a central point for the city of Paris. A bronze column was raised in the center of the square, and this is now the rallying point for the large popular processions that give rhythm to the life of this democracy.

A brand new opera replaced a train station that was one of the most appreciated stations in Paris, because it took them slowly to the nearby countryside along the Marne and its many *guinguettes*, small restaurants on the banks of the river with music and dancing.

While the destruction of the Bastille was also a symbolic gesture, Paris was the scene of many transformations that were closer to vandalism during the sometimes enthusiastic, sometimes dark days of the Revolution. The authorities in power wanted to destroy anything that bore traces of the now hated and rejected powers of the monarchy and the church.

Religious monuments were attacked as symbols for power, the statues of Notre-Dame de Paris were beheaded, and religious establishments were emptied of their inhabitants and their goods, and were given new and sometimes trivial roles. In this way, the heart of the oldest part of Paris lost what remained of these medieval splendors.

While this destruction was taking place, the Revolution decreed that the Louvre would serve a new purpose: it was to be the Museum of the Arts. The

The Bastille column seen through the curves of the Art Deco metro entrance designed by Guimard.

The massive shape of the Conciergerie has preserved part of its medieval origins. Great modifications, which changed the original monument, were progressively made. The Tour de l'Horloge (Clock Tower) on the left was built in 1353. The clock that gives it its name was commissioned by Charles V and the bas-reliefs surrounding it were made by Germain Pilon. It suffered a great deal of damage during the vandalism of the Revolution, and was restored in 1849.

artistic treasures of the Crown were gathered there, as well as spoils coming from the homes of many emigrants, and the idea of the grandiose Louvre museum was prepared. This would reach its peak under Napoléon, thanks to the spoils of war that saw treasures taken from the losers and brought back to Paris. When this artistic booty arrived triumphantly in Paris, ceremonies were held which resembled the processions of conquerors in ancient Rome.

Through a series of decrees, the Convention created the Natural History Museum on the site of the former King's Garden (today the Jardin des Plantes), and the Musée des Arts et Métiers (the Museum of Arts and Trades) was founded in one of the oldest religious establishments of Paris, the convent of Saint-Martin-des-Champs.

Even more surprising, and due to the private initiative of an amateur archeologist, a charming figure from this period, the Musée des Monuments Français (the French Monument Museum) was created in the old Petits Augustins convent, which had been created by Queen Margot in her palace on the left bank (this is now the École des Beaux-Arts, the School of Fine Arts). Alexandre Lenoir managed to save scraps from the hands of vandals during the vast campaign of destruction, and gathered a collection of tombs, recumbent effigies, statues, and miscellaneous works, creating a garden which would become the birthplace of romantic thought, with the attractive name of the Jardin Élyséen (the Elysian Garden). He also "invented" the tomb of Héloïse and Abelard, which was later moved to the Père-Lachaise cemetery.

The deep marks left in the Parisian landscape by the Revolution are spread over a surface which corresponds to the size of the city at the time, and reaches out to the territories that were partly fallow at the place de la Nation (which had been called the place du Trône, the square of the Throne, and after the Revolution was called the place du Trône Renversé, the square of the Overturned Throne). The current square contains a haughty sculpture by Dalou: *Triumph of the Republic*, which looks far off to the west, the direction that Paris has always looked toward since its beginning. This is a symbolic monument, which leads the entire city in its triumphant march.

Nearby, away from the sounds of traffic, in the tranquillity of a tiny cemetery, at 35 rue de Picpus, is one of the most secret parts of Paris, a place where the dead were buried hastily when there had been a guillotine on the square. In this carefully maintained cemetery are many people including André Chenier, and many aristocrats of a France that was torn apart, as well as the tomb of Marquis de La Fayette, which is piously honored every year by the American community. This nobility also has another burial ground, a place of contemplation and reverence on the boulevard Haussmann, in what has become the square Louis XVI. Buried here are the victims of the guillotine when it was on the place de la Concorde, and this includes such famous names as Charlotte Corday, the Brissot deputies, Vergniaud, Philippe-Égalité, Olympe de Gouges, and even Louis XVI himself and Marie-Antoinette. His successor, Louis XVIII, in a diplomatic act of piety, had an expiatory chapel built by the architect Fontaine, containing the mausoleums of the royal couple sculpted by Bosio and Cortot. For a final pilgrimage to the land of the dead, we can go to the tiny cemetery adjoining the Sainte-Marguerite church, where the remains of the Dauphin Louis XVII are buried.

The Conciergerie, which is part of the Palais de Justice on the île de la Cité, has hardly been changed since it was transformed into a prison. It has come through the centuries, since its medieval origins, and the painful saga of the Revolution, when it was the antechamber for death and the condemned would leave the court of May toward the place de la Concorde by a path that followed the rue Saint-Honoré. Many houses along this street still date back to this period.

Utopias of a Royal Reign

The palaces of the Roi de Rome, the rue de Rivoli and the place de l'Étoile

The place du Châtelet was built on the site of the old Châtelet, a fortress, which gave it its name. The original Châtelet was built to defend the bridge giving access to the île de la Cité. At first it was a simple wooden building, and then in 1130 a strong stone building was built. When the city wall was built by Philip Augustus, it had lost its defensive role, but it became the seat of jurisdiction of the Provost of Paris. It was demolished in 1802, and changed into a square, which was later extended, and took on its definitive shape in 1858. This period saw the destruction of a maze of small streets around it, including the rue de la Vieille-Lanterne where Gérard de Nerval hung himself. The fountain was also moved to its current location. It was made by Bralle, and is dominated by a Victory statue by Boizot, who also sculpted the four figures surrounding its base: Faith, Strength, Law, and Vigilence. The two theaters (Théâtre du Châtelet and Théâtre de la Ville) frame this square in majestic equilibrium.

The place de la Concorde. The view up to the Madeleine is similar to that across the Seine of the Palais-Bourbon, which houses the French Assemblée Nationale (the Parliament). These two facades look on each other as if in mirrors.

Of all the rulers who truly wanted to enlarge and embellish Paris, Napoléon I was the first to have a larger, and, above all, more unitary view of this question. When he was very young he said, "If I were to rule France, I would want to make Paris not only the most beautiful city that was, but also the most beautiful city that could ever be." When he rose to power, he was able to do his best to realize this dream. But the series of wars he embarked on, and the huge expenses they required, tempered this original vision. In 1807, five years after he was crowned but already so close to his fall (in 1815), his administration took stock of the situation. Work was being done on the facade of the Palais Bourbon, the Marché des Jacobins (Saint-Honoré), the new cemeteries (Père-Lachaise), and a series of fountains (the allée Saint-Sulpice); and there was more work to be done: the Halle aux Blés (the wheat market), the Tribunal du Commerce (the business court), the place du Châtelet, and the completion of the place Saint-Sulpice and the place de l'Observatoire. These were, however, minor things compared to the larger projects which hallmarked his reign, such as the building of the rue de Rivoli and its arcades, the raising of the Vendôme column, the restoration of the Arc de Triomphe du Carrousel (at the instigation of Vivant Denon, who had accompanied Bonaparte on his campaign to Egypt and would be the designer of his artistic policies), the development of the place de l'Étoile around the Arc de Triomphe, the Temple de la Gloire (the Temple to Glory - the Madeleine), the palais Brongniart (the Paris Bourse), extensions to the Louvre under the direction of Percier and Fontaine, but above all the dream of a palais du Roi de Rome (King of Rome palace) on the Chaillot hill (at the place du Trocadéro) which would have looked out over this quarter which was still almost countryside, and would have been a clear sign of the extension of Paris to the west. When the Empire fell, there was only a foundation for this palace which would soon be covered by ivy and moss." The Cyclopean base of this palace will disappear on its own just as the prince who was to live there disappeared." In the Paris of ghosts, this is a bit like the legend of Babylon. This was too ambitious to be built.

Pages 108-109:
In Men of Good Will, Jules Romains highlights the specific beauty of the Champs-Élysées, "this wide, wide avenue which rises... or rather which moves away and spreads out widely before rising. So wide: could there be another somewhere that is this wide? Its width here is a virtue, a mystery. It is as if the square could not hold itself back, and carries itself away, escaping..."

The Arc de Triomphe du Carrousel is framed by two sentry boxes, which come from the old fence which closed the Cour des Princes in front of the Tuileries palace, and which separated it from the place du Carrousel and the residential quarter there. This Arc de Triomphe was built in 1806-1808. It is the work of two architects from the Louvre: Percier and Fontaine. It was used as a parade entrance to the Tuileries palace.

Victor Hugo, who was profoundly linked to the Arc de Triomphe, lay in state there after his death, dressed in sumptuous clothes but in a pauper's coffin according to his wishes. He had declared "Oh! Paris is the mother city! / Paris is a solemn place / Where the ephemeral whirlwind / Spins around an eternal center! / Paris! Dark fire or pure star! / Gloomy Isis covered by a veil! / Spider with a huge web / Where nations flock! / Fountain of obsessed urns! / Ever overflowing breast / Where generations come / To nourish themselves on its ideas." He was thinking of the Arc de Triomphe. Since that time, another body has been placed there for its eternal sleep: an unknown soldier, for whom the flame burns, and for whom the flags are lowered each night.

A Long, Calm River

The Course of the Seine

*Notre-Dame de Paris.
Mouloudji sang "I miss Paris / When I'm far from here / I feel sad / My heart gets bored / I think of this lady / Whose beaming roofs / Around Notre-Dame / Make infinite waves."*

Victor Hugo drew his inspiration from the Notre-Dame cathedral when he wrote his book The Hunchback of Notre-Dame. *This is a novel about Esmeralda and Quasimodo; Quasimodo's character was inspired by the expressive character of the different sculpted figures on the cathedral where all types of people can be seen.*

*Pages 114-115:
Aragon must have been thinking of the île Saint-Louis when he wrote: "Do you know the island / In the heart of the city / Where all is calm / Eternally / The shadow that rules / Moves there in silence / Like a siren / And its lover / The deep Seine / In its blond arms / In the middle of the world / Hugs it while dreaming."*

Together with the spiraling growth that sees Paris no longer limited to its island, but taking over its surrounding land, a linear dynamic began which followed the course of the Seine. Here, the growth of the city follows the path of the sun, going from east to west, from the Bois de Vincennes to the Bois de Boulogne, from the place de la Nation to the place de l'Étoile, and along this path the city's growth leaves behind a number of landmarks and symbolic monuments that give meaning to it.

The official institutions, the centers of control, were first built on the île de la Cité (the palace of political power, the cathedral) and these would slowly multiply and spread throughout the city. But in no way was this growth arbitrary. There was a certain amount of order behind the installations of the institutions given to the community (for teaching, worship, justice, local power and leisure) and even cultural establishments (museums, libraries, concert halls).

As a counterweight for the palace, which became the Palais de Justice (the courthouse), Notre-Dame cathedral is one of the major landmarks in Parisian itineraries, and its condensed strength shows the energy of Gothic art, of which this is one of the prime examples. The solemnity of its facade was perfect for a building that fit in to the atmosphere of the island, before Haussmann created a parvis in front of it so it could be better admired. This imposing mass has continually been linked to the history of the city. Beneath

The poet O.V. de L. Milosz wandered melancholically along the banks of the île Saint-Louis: "The dead leaves drop in the dormant air / Look, my dear, what autumn has done to your darling island / It is so pale! / What an orphan in peace / The bells ring, they ring at Saint-Louis-en-l'Isle / For the dead fuschia of the woman on the barge."

the ribs of its arch, which had barely been completed, Saint-Louis, in a great gesture of piety, walked barefoot carrying the Crown of Thorns that belonged to Christ, for which he had built the nearby Sainte-Chapelle, a reliquary made of stone and glass; Bossuet spoke here with a firm and threatening voice, cursing the "great lords" whose arrogance he defied with his exemplary Sermons; Napoléon was crowned here in great pomp under the admirative and servile eyes of David, who immortalized the scene in a painting.

A center of great popular gatherings, of celebrations throughout the heroic episodes of the nation's history, this is also a site that inspired romanticized fantasies. When Victor Hugo dedicated one of his greatest works to this cathedral, he made it the setting for a sparkling sentimental novel that prefigured the many popular novels which would be written at the end of the 19th century.

In its wake, as if it were a ship attached to it, the île Saint-Louis is a fine illustration of the calm luxury of the 17th century. Some of this period's most prestigious hôtels were built here, and their inhabitants would be part of the city's cultural life, while they protected themselves, staying almost shut off from the rest of the world, in what was a delightfully provincial manner.

At first this was the Île aux Vaches, the Island of Cows. A bit of land in the center of the city which had been left to the lower classes, who lived a delightful country-like life just a stone's throw away from the ports which spread their services on the right bank from the Grève (the shore), which gave its name to a large square, the place de la Grève (now the place de l'Hôtel de Ville).

The banks of the île Saint-Louis run along an exceptional row of hôtels, most of which date back to the urbanization of the 17th century. "The perimeter of the island could be reserved for nothing other than wandering, relaxing, walking", claims Frédéric Vitoux, a resident of the island.

The bouquinistes (second hand booksellers) along the banks of the Seine are a unique feature of Paris. Clément Lepidis, one of Paris' admirable wanderers, wrote of their charm: "No one would even think of taking the bouquinistes off the parapets, they sleep next to their treasure chests where Balzac chats with Chateaubriand, and Céline talks with Rimbaud and San-Antonio." Charles Nodier, when he was an administrator for the Arsenal Library, would take a daily walk along both banks of the Seine, from his home at the Arsenal to near the Institut de France. And Anatole France, whose father was a bookseller near the Seine, also had much to say about their strange attraction.

Strictly a foot bridge, the Pont des Arts makes it possible to cross quickly from the left bank (rue de Seine) to the Louvre quarter (which is where it gets its name from: the Bridge of the Arts). It is located along a line that runs up to the Cour Carrée giving a sober view. The first version of this bridge dates back to 1801. It was damaged in 1971 by a river barge, and for many years was unusable. It has since been restored and enlarged. Along the bridge are benches and trees in planters, and a crowd of wanderers and painters come here to see one of the most extraordinary points of view of Paris in the heart of its river.

Restif de la Bretonne, one of these prodigious Parisian saunterers who wrote some of the most important texts on daily life in the city, full of anecdotes and sometimes mischievous, often came to this island in the middle of the 18th century, which was a time of one of the greatest revolutions of thought. This gallant wanderer would write the names of the women he loved on the parapets of the quays that surrounded the island. He loved many women, and was the first to brand the island with a sign of charm and casualness. Then there was the rediscovered luxury of the hôtel de Lauzun, which was, in Baudelaire's time, a meeting place for bohemians. It was the "club des Haschichins" who would smoke this drug together and praise it.

At the bow of the island, meeting the waters which break at the tip of a square dedicated to the memory of the sculptor Barye, used to stand the hôtel de Bretonvilliers, of which the only remaining trace is an arch spanning over the modest street which bears its name. This was one of the most admired residences in

They drift by, slow and solemn in the middle of the river, they hide under the arches of the bridges and enchant passersby: these are the many boats that attract crowds because they give the best and most charming view of a relaxed Paris. This is the Paris of the river, where restrained monuments unfold like pictures in a book as you flow by slowly.

Hardly any more bouquinistes sell rare books, such as those discovered by the bibliophiles of the 19th century. Charles Monselet, a friend of Baudelaire, was a model for this. But you now find piles of old mystery books, and the surprising charm of a few books that bring back childhood memories and the first discoveries of reading.

The Pont Marie owes its name to its promoter. It was built in 1630 and Louis XIII laid down the first stone. After being partially destroyed, it was restored in 1670, and the houses on the bridge were progressively removed. The bridge was totally cleared in 1780. It was at this point that a chain was strung between the Loriaux and Barbeau towers of the Charles V wall, before the bridge was built. This was a way of preventing invaders from coming down the river, which had often been the case during the early history of Lutetia.

Along the banks of the river, could they be humming a song by Léo Ferré: "I drank Paris / With a gloomy voice / Along the streets / We sing / There is no hope / In your rags / Only the pavement / But it's so good / Your vagabonds / Make scenes / But under the bridges / Flows the Seine / For romance / To illusion / We're not alone / But it's so good"

A stairway going down to the banks of the Seine. Baudelaire wrote of them: "The shivering dawn in a gown of green and rose, / Advanced slowly along the deserted Seine, / And a darkened Paris, while rubbing its eyes, / Grasped its tools, a hard-working old man."

A flea market along the banks of the Seine. Bringing back memories of the wanderer along both banks that Guillaume Apollinaire talked

Paris is also a port. There were times when there were so many different types of ships in the river that the Seine was congested. Boats are rarer today, but they bring the colors of many horizons. The Seine has its floating exoticism.

For a long time money was struck in different parts of Paris (the Palais de la Cité, the rue de la Vieille Monnaie, the Louvre) before Louis XV decided to built an hôtel which was worthy of these symbols. He bought it from the prince de Conti, who lived at the Temple because he served as its prior. Louis XV asked Jacques-Denis Antoine to build the Hôtel de la Monnaie that we see there today. This was the beginning of the Louis XVI style.

Pages 124 and 125:
*The Alexandre III Bridge was built for the 1900 World Exhibition, and it was czar Nicolas II who lay the first stone in 1896. This was a technical exploit, and the bridge contains splendid decorations in the style of the times. The supporting pillars (right bank) are framed by allegorical sculptures by Frémiet (*The Fame of Science *and* The Fame of the Arts*): at the base is a statue called* Contemporary France *by Gustave Michel and* Charlemagne's France *by Alfred Lenoir, together with stone lions by Pierre Granet; on the left bank,* The Fame of Re-emerging France *by Jules Coutan and* The France of Louis XIV *by Laurent Marqueste with stone lions by Dalou. This is an anthology of "fin de siècle" sculpture in its expressive scale and panache.*

Paris, and its interior decoration had been entrusted to Simon Vouet, Mignard and Bourdon.

Nearby is the hôtel Lambert, which was a model for some of the greatest artists of the 17th century, including Le Brun and Le Sueur.

The former Louviers Island, which no longer exists, having been joined to the mainland on the right bank, was a fallow field for a long time, and was later used as a wood depot. Victor Hugo used a tavern there, frequented by workers and thieves, as the setting for his play *The King Amuses Himself*.

At the western tip of the île Saint-Louis, coming up against the chevet of Notre-Dame, there are beautiful panoramic views of the course of the river. It was here that Apollinaire, the bard of Paris who is present at every street corner, came to contemplate the wavering reflections of the streetlights in the water.

Continuing downstream, after the interlude of the Palais de Tokyo with its 1937 World Exhibition ornamentation, and the Palais de Chaillot (formerly the Palais de Trocadéro), is a smaller artificial island whose sharp edge runs along the Quai de Passy, connecting the Bir-Hakeim bridge to the Quai de Grenelle, across from the Maison de la Radio. This is the Île aux Cygnes (Swan Island), an allusion to the island a little bit further upstream which was connected to the mainland (like Louviers Island) during urban development.

At the tip of this island is the *Statue of Liberty*, a small replica of the statue that Bartholdi made for the city of New York. While it is little more than a small walking path along the Seine, the Île aux Cygnes is nonetheless a charming spot to wander, one of the many surprising areas that can be found in Paris.

The walk along the edge of the Seine has changed its appearance many times, before its uniformization, and the creation of a rivalry with a footpath which is constantly assaulted by automobile traffic, which has been partly restricted to the express roads, which give

At the tip of the île des Cygnes (Swan Island), is a copy of the Statue of Liberty by Bartholdi, looking out toward the hills of Saint-Cloud. This artificial island takes its name from the island that was across from the quai Branly. It was a series of small islets (l'île des Treilles, l'île aux Vaches, l'île de Longchamp) which had been called the îles Maquerelle. Louis XIV brought swans to swim in the Seine, which is where its name comes from. It was connected to the left bank during the First Empire, and the street of the same name was created in 1825. It is connected to the Bir-Hakeim Bridge, and the RER suburban train bridge crosses it in the middle and goes slowly uphill toward the pont de Grenelle. The Front de Seine quarter is one of Paris' major architectural projects of recent years. It was a rundown working-class quarter, and some seedy cafés and dance halls attracted an unruly crowd. Jean Lorrain, who wandered here during its more squalid times, knew this area well and wrote some picturesque descriptions of it.

This quarter, where the Statue of Liberty and the pont de Grenelle blend into the twilight, was the heart of the automobile industry at the beginning of the century. The land taken over from these factories now has new functions (the Citroën Park, the Maison de la Radio).

drivers and passengers some of the most charming points of view in Paris (near the Institut de France and the islands). These footpaths give the stroller a chance to contemplate, from below, the most interesting bridges that punctuate this route from Auteuil to Bercy, with some moments of exceptional beauty such as the Pont-Neuf and the Pont Marie, its nearby neighbor.

For a long time the banks of the Seine were nothing but a sloped shore where warehouses, ports and bathing houses were built over the years. As work went on to progressively develop the quays, it became a more attractive place to walk. While in the 17th century it was chic to be seen riding in horse-drawn coaches along the Cours-la-Reine (from the place de la Concorde to the place de l'Alma), the 19th century saw the creation of strolling. What is more, the stalls of the *bouquinistes* created a race of walkers who were both wise and curious, and who browsed with pleasure, such as Charles Nodier, who, when he was the administrator of the Arsenal library, took a daily walk along both sides of the Seine going as far as the Pont Royal. Another famous stroller was Anatole France, whose father had a bookshop on the Quai Voltaire, and Guillaume Apollinaire gave this activity its letters patent of nobility, by writing its bible: *Walks along Both Banks*.

Romantic Escapades

The Nouvelle-Athènes quarter

Many ghosts from the past can be found in the Nouvelle-Athènes quarter. George Sand crossed Alfred de Vigny, Théophile Gautier, Gérard de Nerval, Chopin as well as Delacroix. The time that has flowed along these streets has conserved something of their prestigious past.

The 19th century saw the development of some new quarters built along the old ramparts built by Louis XIII and around the outside of the boulevards. The quarter that was closest to the boulevards was the Chaussée-d'Antin quarter, which takes its name from the main road which was a fashionable place to live during the Empire. It was in this quarter, in a house near what is now the rue de Provence, that Napoléon spent his years as a young lover with Josephine, and prepared his coup d'état. The Porcherons quarter around the Trinité church, a working class quarter of market gardeners, became middle class in the 19th century. The slightly sloping streets that led to the Butte Montmartre left from here (rue de Clichy, rue Blanche and rue Pigalle). They also surrounded this Nouvelle-Athènes which was limited to a few streets (rue La Rochefoucauld, rue Tour-des-Dames, rue Notre-Dame-de-Lorette, rue Saint-Georges) which, from the years of romanticism through the impressionist period, would be filled with all the key figures of cultural life.

Many romantics lived here: near the Cour d'Orléans (where George Sand and Chopin lived during their tumultuous love affair), in the rue Chaptal, in what has become the Musée de la Vie Romantique (Museum of Romantic Life) at number 16, which was where the painter Ary Scheffer, who attracted the intelligentsia of the time, lived and worked; the rue de la Tour-des-Dames, which is still delightfully provincial even now, and which is where Mademoiselle Mars, an actress who specialized in roles from Marivaux and Molière, lived at number 1; the legendary tragic actor Talma (at number 9), who was greatly admired by Napoléon; the painters Horace Vernet and his son-in-law Paul Delaroche who was famous especially for his painting The Assassination of duc de Guise (at number 7). It was on the rue La Rochefoucauld, at number 14, that the painter Gustave Moreau built the studio-museum which is today dedicated to his work, and on the corner of the rue Fontaine, Gavarni had his own studio - he was very appreciated by the Goncourt brothers who liked the lively caustic style of this type of chronicler of his time. It is significant that a few steps from there, rue Notre-Dame-de-Lorette, Delacroix had his studio at 58 and that Gauguin was born at number 56 in 1848. The Impressionists would soon replace the Romantics.

Megalomania

Napoléon III and Haussmann

Annexation Decree by Adolphe Yvon (Musée Carnavalet), a painting which symbolizes the unification of Paris with its nearby faubourgs, *transforming them into arrondissements. Napoléon III's program for the urbanization of Paris was the most ambitious of all those that had been imagined by French leaders throughout the centuries. Its engineer was baron Haussmann. Modern Paris was born of this.*

The touching pictures taken by Marville and Atget, which are often reproduced and are quite well known today, show the charm of Paris at a time when part of it was still countryside, with skewed views, fallow areas, quirky angles, and modest houses. These houses were poor, but they were so closely a part of their milieu that they give us a feeling of serenity, as if time had stopped. This Paris survived in spite of the large construction projects that were always fragmented and interrupted, and which maintained whole portions of the city in constant growth. The Haussmann plan, following orders from Napoléon III, would wipe the calm pastoral Paris completely off the map. This was all done in the name of modernity, but with a hidden desire to subjugate the crowds. The Medieval remnants of Paris that had been conserved favored the many riots that occurred here, and for a ruler who wanted to avoid this inconvenience, it was clear that this radical urbanization project, which considered the city as a whole (which was an entirely new concept), was necessary.

Haussmann cut gashes in the urban fabric that were so radical that he was jeered by public opinion. The boulevards, avenues and streets which were created in the name of efficiency totally changed the face of the capital: boulevard Saint-Germain, boulevard Sébastopol, boulevard Malesherbes, boulevard Saint-Michel, boulevard Voltaire, boulevard Magenta, boulevard Arago, boulevard du Palais, boulevard Ornano, boulevard Henri-IV, boulevard Raspail,

boulevard Saint-Marcel and boulevard de La Tour-Maubourg; avenue de l'Opéra, avenue Victoria, avenue Parmentier, avenue de Friedland, avenue d'Iéna, avenue de l'Alma, avenue Bosquet and avenue de la République; rue de Rivoli, rue des Écoles, rue de Maubeuge, rue Turbigo, rue Claude-Bernard, rue Lafayette, rue des Pyrénées, rue Réaumur and rue de Rennes, and some squares like the place de l'Opéra, place de l'Hôtel de Ville, place de la République, as well as the square in front of Notre-Dame.

A surgical program was undertaken to improve traffic flow, and to soon welcome the automobile. This also led to the construction, and its phenomenon of real estate speculation, of many buildings that met new standards of hygiene. Haussmann gave a new face to the streets of Paris.

Impressionist painters were the first to realize the importance of this, and photography would assert its power, which would never be refuted, of giving the best visual and graphical records. This was done either by glorifying cold beauty or capturing what could escape from it, which is usually a normal reflex of opposition. This helped create the myth of a country-like working class Paris, which survived as if by a miracle, and which would continue through Brassaï and Doisneau, Cartier-Bresson and Prévert, the films of Marcel Carné and realistic songs. This was a Paris that resisted. It was the same one that made a hero of Gavroche, and made "Titi", the Parisian urchin, a legendary character.

The île de la Cité was disemboweled by Haussmann. In order to rehabilitate the île de la Cité, and improve access to the island, baron Haussmann destroyed the center, which was a clutter of shops, buildings and houses, some of which dated back to the Middle Ages. He wished to build an administrative city here. He started by moving the Hôtel-Dieu, which was on the right side of Notre-Dame, and giving it a larger space on the north side of the island. The traditional housing of the island was replaced by administrative buildings. More recent works, on the parvis in front of Notre-Dame, have led to the discovery and presentation of the foundations of the original Paris. This is the archeological crypt of Notre-Dame.

Double page overleaf:
Aerial view of the Champs-Élysées quarter. The mark left by Haussmann's work can be seen all over Paris. He gave the city a structure with its large avenues, he developed many of its monuments, giving a certain scale to the buildings of the city. He invented a Paris that is less that of prestige than of luxury, and an art de vivre which is recognized all around the world.

Paris Walks

The Pont-Neuf, the Galerie du Palais, the place Royale and the Boulevards

Along the rue de Rivoli, along the Tuileries, in the garden of the Palais-Royal, and all around it, are arcades protecting strollers from bad weather. They are part of an urban tradition which came from Italy, and which fits in perfectly with vast urban development projects that give priority to people.

A (contested) program was carried out, whose goal was to assimilate contemporary art with classical architecture. The modern rhythms of Buren's columns serve as a counterpoint to the strict colonnades of the Palais Royal.

When the Pont-Neuf was built, it was immediately adopted by the Parisian lower classes as a place for taking walks. Located in the middle of a triangle, made up by the Louvre, les Halles, the Hôtel de Ville and the Palais de Justice, it attracted large crowds. The racket in the middle of the road was unbelievable, there were strolling actors, charlatans, criers, merchants and bandits, which were among the most active of the different professions represented, and which were the scourge of Paris which was still dangerous at night and a den of thieves.

The diversity of trades and social classes that met here remains unique in the history of Paris walks. The bridge progressively lost its exclusiveness and attraction, but this took quite some time. Other areas would then suddenly become popular. The first of these places, whose location did not inspire the same debauchery, was the shopping arcades of the Palais de Justice that were very popular in the 17th century. The shops that were there extolled the quality of their products and selected a clientele that could honor them. There was a long parade of well-dressed lords and ladies in lace who would come here to look for imported clothes and books. The exquisite etchings of Abraham Bosse have immortalized these lords leaving the hôtel de Rambouillet. They wore large feathered hats, flowing coats, highwayman's boots and wore that "beard of respect" which replaced the pointy beard that had been worn by all of the Henri III's Court. This was a chattering, boasting group of people that would be depicted in the swashbuckling novels of Alexandre Dumas, giving such a picturesque image of Paris under Louis XIII and during Louis XIV's childhood.

Carrying the weight of its years, the Pont-Neuf (the New Bridge, here with floral decorations designed by Kenzo) is, in spite of its name, the oldest bridge in Paris. For a long time it was a street theater, the preferred stage for strolling actors and tricksters.

When the Tuileries was built, its surrounding area was developed along with its garden, and beyond what was still just empty land (what would become the place de la Concorde), a bridle path was made. This path went all the way to the hills of Saint-Cloud, and was frequented by the coaches of the beautiful and the gallant returning from the boudoirs of Ninon de Lenclos or Marion Delorme.

They held court in the new hôtels on the place Royale (now the place des Vosges) which was very fashionable then. Its arcades encouraged intrigue, but also prostitution, which would later move toward the Palais Royal when the architect Louis built arcades there for the duc D'Orléans. This was then the fashionable spot. It remained so until the Directory. Its functions remained the same, the only things that changed were the costumes, which tended to become lighter, representing a desire for emancipation that followed the darkest days of the Terror.

This hustling, useless, talkative crowd full of simple minded people emigrated toward the Grands Boulevards as their construction increased. These boulevards, built along the former location of Louis XIII's city wall, would become the showcase for business, politics, letters and gallantry in Paris.

Burned down during the Commune, the Tuileries palace, which stood between the two pavilions (the pavillon de Marsan and the pavillon de Flore) was destroyed, to give the Louvre more space. The space was used for gardens, containing sculptures by Maillol, for a long time. Many major changes in the development of the Grand Louvre turned this into an esplanade designed to highlight the central pyramid.

The place des Vosges, formerly called the place Royale, was a center for gallantry. Marion Delorme had her salon here, where Parisian high society came to visit her. An expert in this domain, Romi, in In Love with Paris, said "Now the place Royale will soon become the meeting place for the high society, the fashionable place to stroll, the center of elegance in Paris. This is where women of society will come to be seen."

The place des Vosges again has a normal neighborhood life, and there are many picturesque antique shops and quiet restaurants which use the arcades to make pleasant terraces. People come with their entire families to look for bargains. Léon-Paul Fargue wandered here: "Now the place des Vosges is nothing more than a refuge for fortune tellers, small gunsmiths, usurers and attorneys. The place Royale and the streets of the Marais were abandoned by the middle-classes. The shadows of thieves run along the walls, the same walls that used to bear the shadows of horse-drawn coaches. Women with wide shoulders, and greasy hair, who come down on the sidewalk with their chairs and sweaters, have invaded this charming place where we used to write poetry when we weren't fighting duels..." But Fargue wrote this in the 1930s. This quarter has become fashionable again since then.

Le Fouquet's.
In 1899, Louis Fouquet bought a restaurant that was frequented by the coachmen of fiacres who brought their customers to the bois de Boulogne. His successor imitated Maxim's by adding the "'s", to make it sound English, at a time when Britain was very popular. Simenon wrote of his emotions when he discovered this café upon his arrival in Paris: "There it was, in the silent world where all you could hear were the steps of a few rare horses pulling fiacres, this was the famous heart of Paris that the starved young man that I was had dreamed of."

An exhibit on the Champs-Élysées. This tree-lined avenue is perfect for this sort of temporary sculpture exhibit, which is always a great popular success. In the foreground, a sculpture by Niki de Saint-Phalle.

Fortifications and Empty Land

The Thiers Fortifications

> There still remain a few towers from the wall of Philippe Augustus, which are hidden behind buildings (the passage du Commerce), courtyards, streets and even a parking lot (rue Mazarine). Here, in memory of this wall, an elegant brick tower was built on the rue des Francs-Bourgeois.

Paris has always confined itself within the limits of a protecting wall. At its birth, when it was still Lutetia, it built walls, although the island's position should have been sufficient for its protection. When the city spread to both banks of the river, a first wall was built (the Philip Augustus wall) which was quickly seen to be too small. After this a series of defending walls were built, and each of them extended the territory of the city without changing its overall shape. The Charles V wall (part of it can be seen in the shopping gallery of the Grand Louvre) was itself included in the wall built by Louis XIII.

The Mur des Fermiers Généraux (the Farmers General wall), this "wall surrounding Paris which made Paris surround itself" included pavilions designed by Claude Nicolas Ledoux. To replace the old fortified gates, which were strictly used for military defense, new gates were used to mark the border between taxed areas and free areas. Because of this, a lasting tradition developed where a group of poor people would camp near the city walls. The building of the Thiers Fortifications, which no longer served a purpose after the events of 1870, was a proof of this, and many literary accounts remain describing this atmosphere.

Just like the banks of the Seine, the "forts" were a Sunday Eldorado for the lower classes. In *Germinie Lacerteux*, the Goncourt brothers give a pleasant description: "The air was full of organ music. Below her, in the ditch, groups of people played in all four corners. Out in front of her there was a motley crowd; there were white shirts, children with blue aprons running around, cafés, wine shops, fried food stands, ring toss games, shooting ranges half hidden in a bouquet of plants where masts with tricolor flames rose." Zola, the people's bard, had his characters spend time there. This was "the place to walk for working-class and lower middle-class people". J. K. Huysmans, in *Sketches of Paris*, praised "the wonderful and terrible view" or "the sincere spectacle of this suburb celebrating", specifying that "for people for whom the constant greed of tradesmen suffice, this atmosphere which comes from the suburb becomes entertaining and relaxing, combined with the excitement of children set free, exhilarated by a bit of fresh air".

This continued until Jean Lorrain, who often wandered in these rough areas, praised the strange and dangerous people who haunted this fallow place.

This line of walls and outposts containing towers, chicanes, moats and other defensive structures, which are large construction projects, constantly add to this growing city uncertain areas whose functions are not defined, that can not be lived in, and that are often converted into vegetable gardens or empty lots. The neighboring people improvised a certain idea of nature, which corresponded to their limited means, also because these lands were always more or less temporary. It recalls the common practice in the 19th century of creating improvised gardens along the edges of railways, which decorated the right of way with this naive beauty of a kind of nature which is to the French gardens of the rich neighborhoods, what art brut is to the art seen in museums. This is the Paris of secret gardens, of discreet enclaves where plants fulfill fantasies which are forbidden everywhere else.

Parks and Gardens

From the Tuileries garden to the parc Monceau

This café in the jardin de Luxembourg is a people's version of the "follies" which decorated philosophers' gardens in the 18th century, among false ruins, Turkish tents, and tea palaces. These cafés, like the bandstands that are seen in some gardens, have a fragile mannered style of architecture surrounded by lackadaisical tables, which can often be seen in impressionist paintings.

A puppet show in the garden of Luxembourg. Puppet shows in Parisian parks, such as the one here in the jardin de Luxembourg, are fond memories for the many people who discovered cops and robber stories or fairy tales in these small wooden booths during their childhood.

From the Tivolis of yesteryear to the parks of today, the presence of nature in Paris is a story of pleasure. The arguments put forth by health and hygiene specialists in the 19th century, which are basically the same as those heard today, pleaded for a development of parks which would be open to all. This was not always the case. For the lower-classes, nature was improvised in areas that were forgotten or neglected by buildings. For a long time these spaces were fields or empty lots, which were havens for thieves, and where a world on the fringe organized and grew. Gardens were originally highly civilized spaces reserved for a selected public. Those who wished to go into aristocratic gardens open to the public had to dress correctly in such a way that the morality of other visitors was not shocked.

While Paris was confined within its walls, religious congregations moved in, built and fertilized the ground. They each created their own *enclos* (a closed plot of land), with familiar names: Sainte-Geneviève, Saint-Germain-des-Prés, Saint-Martin-des-Champs, Saint-Jacques, Saint-Victor, and the Chartreux convent. Some of these have disappeared, and others have undergone major changes, but they helped decide what the very shape of the city would be.

While the Champs-Élysées is used to display modern sculptures, the Tuileries garden is a permanent sculpture museum with works by Maillol (such as the one shown below), Coysevox, Coustou, François Barois, Jules Desbois, Pradier, Laurent Marqueste, Auguste Cain, and Carrier-Belleuse.

The poet Alphonse Esquiros declaimed a poem to celebrate the Médicis fountain: "Here in Luxembourg there is an old fountain / I love this monument of uncertain origins / And near a wooden bench, where any may sit / A vague feeling brings the evening back to me."

As Paris grew, it also set aside some fallow areas, some of which would become gardens and would be the first "lungs" of a city which would soon need them.

The construction of the Tuileries palace, outside of the city wall, was a royal whim. But it helped incite the development of land to the west of the city, and by a series of appropriations, would create the famous view that we know today. The Tuileries garden was originally a strictly private area; it was reserved for the inhabitants of the château, and it was the stage for their feasts and spectacles.

Its history corresponds to the evolution of the art of gardens, from the precious squares of the Renaissance up to the noble views of Le Nôtre. It was significant that even though the ruler who lived in the Tuileries palace gave limited access to the public, he reserved for his own use the part of the garden which adjoined it.

After the Tuileries, it was the Palais Royal that saw the construction of a garden, which was later closed off when galleries to extend the palace were added, surrounding the garden, by a member of the Orléans family, and this gave the garden the shape we still know today, and which gives it its charm.

The Luxembourg palace was also built on a royal whim, and the land around it was also appropriated. It was originally much larger than it is today, but it was split up by real estate developments in the 19th century.

The Monceau Park, which was requested by a prince of the Orléans family, was a model for a certain style of 18th century romantic gardens, with a wide scattering of follies, temples, false ruins, and Chinese pagodas. Today, only a few scraps remain in this park, but which makes them that much more precious.

The rich aristocratic hôtels of the Faubourg Saint-Germain, the Faubourg Saint-Honoré and the Marais each had gardens which resembled their promoters, but which also fit in with the current fashion. Many of theses gardens remain, often hidden from the street, such as the garden of the Élysée palace at 55 Faubourg Saint-Honoré, which is open to invited guests on the 14th of July; at 57 rue de Varenne, the garden of the Matignon palace, the largest private park in Paris; at 14 rue Saint-Dominique, which belonged to Napoléon's mother, and has since become the residence of the Minister of War.

At 77 rue de Varenne, access to the garden of the old hôtel Biron has been possible since Rodin had his studio here. His secretary was the poet Rainer-Maria Rilke, and Jean Cocteau lived here for a while as well.

Théophile Gautier often walked along the paths of the jardin de Luxembourg where "happy flocks of sparrows twittered".

He left a surprising description of the way it was back then: "Paris lived, walked, moved, worked, drove around such a silence which is the privilege of parks that have been abandoned… The moonlight came and left its sheets, its statues, its penguins, and its dead nuns. An amazing mass of rubble and wild rose bushes gave off pleasant smells, tangled among a labyrinth of sand and weeds…"

Many of the sculptor's works can be admired today in this same place, including *The Burghers of Calais*, and, especially, *The Gates of Hell*, this ambitious statue with allusions to Dante.

Another discreet garden, which is open to the public, is at the Mission Étrangère, 128 rue du Bac. Chateaubriand could look out over the foliage from his window at 120 rue du Bac. The Babylone garden, 33 rue de Babylone, still has the quiet charm of its origins. It ends with a bower of grapevines, which leads to a pious statue. Another garden that is discreet, delightful and a nice place to go with families, is the Montmartre garden (14 rue Cortot), which is a reminder that this spot was once countryside. Gérard de Nerval spoke of the charm that this space was able to maintain in spite of the odd buildings built around it during the 19th century, buildings that were built chaotically and out of personal interest.

Near the enclos Saint-Victor is the Jardin des Plantes, which had been the King's garden, founded by the doctor-botanist Jean Hérouard, physician to Louis XIII, who has left behind an astonishing journal about the childhood of his king. Jussieu, Daubenton, Lacépède, Geoffroy Saint-Hilaire and Buffon were all curators of this garden, and it became the Museum of Natural History under the Revolution, when its director was Bernardin de Saint-Pierre, the delightful author of *Paul et Virginie*.

It has a long history, and its main purpose was to scientifically gather all known plants. At the beginning, it was only a quarter of its current size, and it was thanks to the dynamic actions of Buffon that it doubled in size and was extended all the way to the Seine. There are many buildings that carry out scientific services and species conservation. A maze leads to a graceful gazebo and a Lebanese cedar tree planted by Jussieu in 1734.

Napoléon III's ambitious policy of urbanization, carried out by baron Hausmann, also had its natural equivalent, under the responsibility of the architect Alphand. He is responsible for many neighborhood squares, which were all designed based on one model that gave priority to decent domestic use by the local population. A rite was born from this, where families take Sunday walks in gardens, and children rule. These squares are decorated by false ponds and patriotic statues, or sculptures dedicated to the myths of the Republic. Here and there, some more surprising squares can sometimes be seen almost by surprise. These were created due to accidents and mistakes in the city's development programs, and are wonderful places to take a stroll.

Hausmann's program was also responsible for some much larger projects, such as the Buttes-Chaumont garden built on what was then just empty land; there were open quarries, rubbish dumps, animals were slaughtered there, and in the midst of this land, the terrible Montfaucon gallows was built, which was immortalized by Villon. The Buttes-Chaumont garden was designed and built to correspond as much as possible to the crazy idea of an idyllic garden. There are crevasses, cliffs and rocks, winding paths along the rocky wild hills; but they're all artificial. The highest point is a re-creation of the temple of Sibyl in Tivoli. This Pirenasi was updated to correspond with ideas from Gothic novels, a delightful "folly". Louis Aragon spoke admirably about walking in this garden, which is one of the most "poetic" gardens in Paris, in *The Night-Walker*.

Haussmann's program for the greening of Paris included two much larger parks that would frame the city. These are the bois de Boulogne and the bois de Vincennes.

What garden or square would be complete without its pool, which is often the main decoration, and its fountain with varying levels of generosity or opulence. The pools of the Tuileries, which date back to Le Nôtre's work in these gardens, were present at some of the great moments of history. The pool at the entrance to the garden (place de la Concorde) was the site of the catafalque built in honor of Jean-Jacques Rousseau when his ashes were transferred to the Panthéon. The pool in the Jardin de Luxembourg has always been associated with Parisian childhood. Many writers, including Gide who lived close by, spoke of their dreams of sailing and the first shudders of the virgin souls that looked out over its water.

Paris is full of pools, ponds and fountains which can be majestic or modest, gentle or spectacular, and which play an active role in a mythology woven under thick beech woods by statues of legendary characters.

Many love affairs were born at the feet of the statues in the jardin de Luxembourg. Many writers have recalled their first loves in the shadows of these queens of France which stand on the terraces of this garden, sculpted by Auguste Ottin, J.B. Klagmann, and Auguste Dumont. There are also statues of many artists and writers such as José Maria de Hérédia, Chopin, Sainte-Beuve, Verlaine, George Sand, Stendhal, Banville, and Murger.

Sometimes used as settings for shows (concerts, fireworks), the central pool of the Tuileries garden is a daily rallying point for junior navigators. Léon Bopp remembers that "on Sundays, hobbyists would come to try out the little steam or gas engine boats that they had made for their children, or for the child that was still a part of them. These inoffensive machines have a certain something that is poetic and reassuring."

The bois de Boulogne, like the bois de Vincennes, is the work of Alphand and was part of a large program to renovate Paris desired by Napoléon III and carried out by Haussmann. It contains all the ingredients needed to enchant the landscape, in the spirit of those 18th century gardens where everything possible was done to uplift the soul. Since the bois de Boulogne was supposed to be a simple place where people would come to play and relax, its allusions were kept simple. It is less philosophic, and is designed only around nature. Water is one of the key elements of this park: it flows, falls (the Grande Cascade), twists and turns, and relaxes, spreading out in a lake with an attractive island in the center, that invites people to take a small boat ride, which is one of the traditional attractions of this park.

With its exceptional location, at the crossroads of several comfortable residential quarters, the highly cultural and peaceful Luxembourg garden sometimes looks like a small local square, with its regulars, including the chess players who come to play long patient games under the cool shade and amidst the playful cries of children.

The time that Rodin spent in what was the Hôtel de Biron (now the Musée Rodin) gave it a vocation, a meaning, and a particular attraction. Memories of this great artist can be seen both inside the hôtel and in its large garden with some of his most famous statues like The Gates of Hell (which can be seen from the street) which was his life's work, and The Thinker, which is one of the main works presented here and the one which made him famous.

City Gates

Gates and Arches

In August Thoughts, *Sainte-Beuve wrote "Breaking with monotonous splendor / The Arc de Triomphe and its darkened walls / Seem to open to the victor of Memphis / Who fills them with the gold of his crown / More than a victor, he is a magi / Who, as he ages, distributes all of his treasure / Or Homère declaiming the Odysee."*

While Paris progressively lost its medieval city gates, its watchtowers, and all the defensive structures that were part of its protecting walls, it started building triumphal gates. Some of these (the Saint-Denis gate and the Saint-Martin gate) were replacements for previous gates that were located at the same spot and which had been used for defensive purposes. These gates were not built to mark new limits to the city, but to be a part of its parade decoration.

The Saint-Denis gate, designed by François Blondel, is decorated with figures by Girardon. These celebrate the glory of Louis XIV after his victory at Maastricht. The custom was that the king would pass through this gate during his triumphal entry into the city.

From Philippe de Valois, Jean Le Bon and Charles V to François I, Henri II and Charles IX, many kings came through the medieval gate, for solemn entrances into the city. Another similar gate is the Saint-Martin gate, built in 1674 by Pierre Bullet, to celebrate the capture of Besançon and the Franche-Comté. Louis XIV is depicted here as Hercules, standing naked, armed with a club.

This idea of an arch of glory was dropped for a while, and then once again became popular under the reign of Napoléon I, who had the Arc de Triomphe du Carrousel and the Arc du Triomphe at the place de l'Étoile built.

The Arc de Triomphe du Carrousel was built by Percier and Fontaine in 1808, and it became the gate of honor to the Tuileries palace. It is a copy of the Roman triumphal arch of Septimus Severus. Its pink Corinthian marble columns come from the old château de Meudon. In 1809, a statue of four horses taken from the San-Marco basilica in Venice was placed on top of the arch, but this was returned after the fall of the empire when its spoils of war were restituted. It was replaced by a wagon pulled by four horses leading the Restoration to glory.

Its distant copy, which can be seen in a beautiful view on a line of sight down the Champs-Élysées, is in the middle of the place de l'Étoile which gives it its name; it was also one of the dreams of triumphal urbanization cherished by Napoléon I. He had selected a spot that had already been developed under Louis XV, when the engineer Ribart de Chamoust had developed a project to build a giant elephant there carrying a statue of the king. Up until the Revolution, there had been thoughts of putting an obelisk there. It was after Napoléon's victory at Austerlitz that he chose this place to build an arch and appointed Chalgrin to build it. He would never see it completed, nor would Napoléon.

Thiers was responsible for completing its decoration, together with Étex, Cortot and, especially, the most famous of the sculptors, Rude, who gave French patriotic history one of its most powerful icons, along with *La Marseillaise*, the French national anthem.

The Arc de Triomphe de l'Étoile is today an integral part of the rites of the Republic, which has buried its unknown soldier there, and uses it as the setting for its military festivities.

The Arc de Triomphe at the place du Trône was one of the dreams of Parisian urbanism. Colbert had already thought about building this, but his project never got beyond initial studies. Claude Nicolas Ledoux, as part of his series of pavilions that punctuated the Farmers General wall, designed a pair of high columns which later saw the addition of statues of Saint-Louis and Philip Augustus.

In its constant progression toward the west, Paris shows off its different types of architecture. Starting with the Renaissance, and its decoration of the Louvre, through the 19th century, which triumphed pompously along the Champs-Élysées, then comes the 20th century, which invented the beauty of light in the strict geometry of the architecture, both refined and megalomaniac, of la Défense and its Grande Arche.

Victor Hugo, among others, spoke of it as a sign of glory: "Paris which holds, without belief / Candles and censers, / In the morning light stands a sign of glory / Which blocks out the sun every night". He was thinking of the Arc de Triomphe, this gate which frames the most beautiful sunsets.

This triumphal way, the Champs-Élysées, goes uphill toward a triumph in the shape of an ancient arch. Here, to celebrate the bicentenary of the French Revolution in 1989, this was a site of huge celebrations. The fireworks are like heavenly jewels.

In spite of the centuries that separate them, the Arc du Triomphe du Carrousel has similarities with the Pyramid at the Louvre. The former was a pastiche of ancient forms as they were imagined under the Empire, and the latter takes its inspiration from this to be modern.

Stages and Footlights

The Châtelet theater, the Opera, theaters, music-halls, and circuses.

The first stone of the Opéra Garnier was laid on July 21st, 1862, but building was slow because of flooding from an underground spring, which would later be the source of a legend that claims that there is a lake underneath the Opera. It was inaugurated in 1875 under the presidency of Mac Mahon. Charles Garnier, its architect, commissioned several artists to decorate the interior of the building, including Falguière, Paul Dubois, Henri Chapu, and especially Jean-Baptiste Carpeaux, whose famous Danse has become the very symbol of choreographic art. At this time, the ceiling was painted by Lenepveu. In the 1960s, under the initiative of André Malraux, then Minister of Culture, it was repainted by Chagall, and at the same time Malraux asked André Masson to repaint the ceiling of the théâtre de l'Odéon.

Theater in cities was originally an integral part of religious life. It took place in churches, and presented a repertoire which followed the principles passed down by the leaders of society, although farces, which were very important in medieval culture, were growing in popularity. When the theater left the church, it was either performed in the street or in fairs (such as the Saint-Germain fair), while the aristocracy had its own more private and selective form of theater. Plays were performed in the hôtel de Sens, the hôtel de Bourbon (in the Cour Carrée of the Louvre), the collège de Beauvais, the collège d'Harcourt, the collège de Clermont, the collège de Cluny and the collège de Navarre.

The Confrères de la Passion (Brotherhood of the Passion) purchased a plot of land (23 rue Étienne-Marcel), which belonged to the hôtel de Bourgogne, in order to build a theater. They used this name for their theater. At the same time, young theater companies were giving performances in *jeux de paumes* (the precursors of tennis courts). It was in the *jeu de paume* near the hôtel de Nesle (rue Mazarine), then later in one near the hôtel de la Croix Noire (32 quai des Célestins), that Molière began performing, and he gave a whole new outlook to the theater.

There was a deep rivalry between the theater at the hôtel de Bourgogne and the one in the Marais (rue Vieille-du-Temple) where Corneille performed, and this rivalry shows how important the theater had become. While a theater with complex machinery was being built at the Tuileries (it was called the Salle des Machines, or the Machinery Room) and at the Palais Royal (by Lemercier), theatrical life was centered around the court of Louis XIV, who brought order and protection to it. Things were organized around Molière. The Comédie-Française (created in 1680) was responsible for most of the theatrical activity which took place first at the hôtel Guénégaud (on the rue Jacques-Callot), then on the rue des Fossés-Saint-Germain (which is now 14 rue de l'Ancienne-Comédie), and finally in a theater that was more adapted to their productions, built by Charles de Wailly (what is now the théâtre de l'Odéon).

The Richelieu theater was built by Louis-Victor Louis, on the orders of a prince of the Orléans family, to hold the Opéra. It burned down in 1781. In 1799, after being rebuilt, it was the theater used by the Society of French Actors. Just like Louis XIV, Napoléon thought that it was important to protect theatrical activity, which was then centered around the mythical figure of Talma.

Theatrical life underwent a great deal of changes, partly due to its popularity, and even though it was supported by those in power, it spread out to more and more theaters. One of these theaters is the salle Favart, built in 1783. It later burned down, and a new theater was built in 1840. Unfortunately, its luck was the same. It burned down again in 1887 and was rebuilt in 1898.

Familiar figures of "Paris by night", ballerinas from the Opéra, were one of the favorite subjects of 19th century painters, from Jean Béraud to Toulouse-Lautrec, not forgetting Degas, whose treatment of this subject was exemplary.

All of the showy luxury of the Second Empire can be seen here. The Opéra entered into social life as an expression of success, and it was the scene of many ostentatious meetings, meant to fuel gossip columns and build reputations. The Opéra was the stage for the human comedy at the time of Nana.

At the same time there were two theaters built opposite each other, along the Seine, in the center of Paris. This is how the Châtelet theater was born (whose name comes from the old medieval Châtelet which was formerly at the same location, and which was a prison), built by Davioud in 1862; the second was the Théâtre Lyrique (the Lyric Theater) which replaced the theater on the boulevard du Temple, which was demolished during Haussmann's rehabilitation of Paris. It had an eventful life, and was even run by Sarah Bernhardt, who gave it her name, before it finally became the Théâtre de la Ville (the Theater of the City) in 1968.

Theaters were built wherever crowds gathered. Since the small theaters on the boulevard du Crime disappeared during the changes of Imperial Paris, the new theatrical center was naturally born along the Grands Boulevards, and at first these theaters were one of the main points of attraction here. A certain form of theater that corresponded to the use of metaphors, which were supposed to reflect the customs of current society, took its name from this location. It was called the *"théâtre de boulevard"*.

The experience of the Palais Garnier is a good example of this supposed relationship between crowds and theaters. By choosing its location in the heart of the boulevards, it was the neighboring quarter that benefited from its presence, with many luxury shops and hôtels being built.

The opera of the rue Le Peletier (which replaced the opera on the rue de Richelieu, destroyed after the duc de Berry was killed there) had just burned down. This was the theater home to the stage and wings which had haunted the painter Degas, together with Halevy, who was to become one of the leading writers of librettos of his time (*La Belle Hélène*, *La Vie parisienne*).

Charles Garnier was asked to build the Opera, and he made it one of the most typical examples of "the Napoléon III style", which was a mixture of different styles, both sumptuous and luxurious, and he relied on the talent of those who were to create the decorations, such as Carpeaux, whose La Danse has become the very symbol of the art of the stage.

In 1990, the Opéra created a second theater at the place de la Bastille, which is a highlight of late 20th century Parisian architecture.

Parisian theater had another adventure related to modern architecture when it was decided to rebuild the Palais de Chaillot, also called the Trocadéro, for the 1937 World Exhibition. On the wings of this building,

The Lido is the last remaining theater with the type of shows which were once very popular on the Champs-Élysées. During the 19th century, Zola, Flaubert, the Goncourt brothers and Maupassant frequented them. Other theaters, such as Les Ambassadeurs, or l'Alcazar d'Eté, were modeled after café-concerts, which Degas appreciated so much. The Lido was created in 1946. Pierre Bost explains what makes it so popular: "A pair of virtuoso dancers, both of them well built, a comedian (indispensable), two honorable or mediocre actors, a naked dancer, and some fancy stage tricks; an "eccentric" dancer or actress; a foreign orchestra, because the grass is always greener, and finally (the main element) a company of well-trained girls. Add to this many extras, lights, and a bit of false poetry…"

sentences are inscribed in golden letters, by the poet Paul Valéry, who was a figurehead of French intellectual life. The company of the Théâtre National de Paris moved in, giving a breath of fresh air to Parisian theater.

To give it the space corresponding to the vision of its position overlooking the city, a long pool was made which leads down toward the Seine. It is surrounded by a group of sculptures, which link the rigor of classicism to the fantasies of modernism.

Degas went often to the Opéra, and, together with his friend Manet, also went to music halls and "more common" theaters. A new type of theater became popular in Paris, where feathers and glitter were the norm. From the Moulin Rouge, popularized by Toulouse-Lautrec, to the Folies Bergère, painted by Manet, there were many theaters which were a part of the Parisian nightlife (Lido, Crazy-Horse, Palace, Paradis Latin) and which played a major role in the image of the city.

The circus, which was a more family oriented type of entertainment, went through successive crises. It lost the Médrano Theater, but managed to conserve the beautiful theater built by Hittorff which was called the cirque Napoléon, where the famous Pasdeloup concerts were also performed. It was later named the cirque d'Hiver (the winter circus) as opposed to the cirque d'Été (the summer circus) which was in the gardens of the Champs-Élysées, and which has since been torn down.

One of the latest large architectural projects of contemporary Paris, the Bastille Opéra, designed by the architect Carlos Ott, was meant to be a popular version of the Opéra Garnier. The old Opera is associated with socialite rites, whereas the new Bastille Opéra is meant to please the masses. Its rigorous architecture is the antithesis of the ostentatious luxury seen in its opposite. It is rational.

Museums of Paris

The Musée Carnavalet, Musée Cernuschi, Musée Grévin, Musée Guimet and the rest

The Hôtel Carnavalet, one of the most famous hôtels in the Marais, was the home to the marquise de Sévigné and members of her family starting in 1677. Today, this hôtel has been changed into a museum dedicated to the memories and relics of the history of Paris. It was enlarged by adding the Hôtel Le Pelletier de Saint-Fargeau to it. Louis-Marie Le Pelletier de Saint-Fargeau, who was a deputy for the nobility at the Estates General, and later a member of the Convention, voted in favor of the death of Louis XVI, and was himself assassinated January 20th, 1793 in the basement of the café Février, in the Palais-Royal.

Both in number and diversity, Parisian museums contain the world's largest collection of objects, memories and works of art, which together help nourish the collective memory of the peoples of the world and raise awareness of universal History.

The history of Paris can be seen in the clearly laid-out sequences at the Musée Carnavalet, whereas the Musée Grévin treats the great moments of History as theatrical scenes, just as school books did in the past, and sometimes honors contemporary figures in a perilous confrontation with characters whose past is glorious and sometimes tragic.

The Musée de l'Armée (Army Museum), in the Hôtel des Invalides, has a collection of weapons from all different periods, and objects relating to Napoléon.

Sometimes ancient buildings reach the present maintaining the unity of ideas which held fast when they were built, and bear witness to the taste of some great collectors of the 19th century: Jacquemart-André (158 boulevard Haussmann), with its profusion of furniture, paintings, and sculptures from the Italian Renaissance to the French 18th century; or Nissim Camondo (63 rue de Monceau), who was more focused on the French 18th century. The collection organized by Cognacq-Jay has recently been installed in a beautiful well-restored old hôtel on the rue Elzévir (at number 8).

Lovers of oriental art will find the memories of Henri Cernuschi in a museum bearing his name (7 avenue Velasquez), across from the green grass and trees of the parc Monceau, while the Musée Guimet, which has been totally renovated (19 avenue d'Iéna), has the most impressive collection of Asian art.

Going further along this foray into arts from "other lands", a stop at the Musée des Arts d'Afrique and d'Océanie (Museum of African and Oeanic Arts, 293 avenue Daumesnil) will help you better understand the evolution of modern art. Works that were so appreciated by Picasso, Braque, Matisse and André Breton, are displayed in an educational setting. Finally, next to the Musée de la Marine (Sea Museum) and its extraordinary ship models, the Musée de l'Homme (Museum of Mankind, Palais de Chaillot) has the most surprising collection of objects and works of art from the civilizations around the world situated in an ethnographic context. This is a scientific view of art.

Villages and Groves

Villa Frochot, Cité Fleurie, Villa Seurat, the Ruche, the Bateau Lavoir

Here and there, forgotten, some quarters of Paris such as Montsouris still look as if they are in the country. As if the city was nothing more than a group of villages stuck together, which slowly gave up their intimacy to the crowds. When discovering some of these Parisian streets that are far from noise and cars, one may have slightly melancholic thoughts. Because it is hard to imagine that they will survive.

Jean Follain, the saunterer inspired by Paris, spoke of the subtle feelings he got during his walks. He told of "these streets with no special charm, no history, that remain somewhat abstract, where night falls more simply, and the hours ring out more distinctly…" Here, a street in the 13th arrondissement.

The survival of different hamlets, villas, and cités (usually small narrow cul-de-sacs, lined with private houses and containing no through streets) in Paris is the consequence of a dismemberment of urban space whose large scale projects often forget entire sections of marginal housing which belongs to the past. These spaces do not fit in with the norms of the city, and are away from the main lines drawn to modernize it. Because of this, they manage to maintain a life style which is very similar to that found in small villages, with a natural friendliness, and a level of greenery much different than elsewhere in the city, where renovated neighborhoods have usually been built of concrete. While this phenomenon is not new, it stands out more today, and the people who live in these areas develop a growing level of prestige from them. These quarters originally contained humble housing, but this has progressively been gentrified and refined as the city around them has grown, threatening these spaces.

Spread out among the city, these preserved spaces have no stylistic unity. Some of them are quite simple (villa Daviel, villa Santos-Dumont, villa Émile-Meyer, la Mouzaïa, villa Manin), and others are affluent and rich in cultural heritage, such as the avenue Frochot, where many famous people lived: Alexandre Dumas (at number 7), Victor Hugo (at number 1), the painter

Isabey (at number 5), Luminais, the painter of the famous painting *The Énervés of Jumièges* (at number 12), Chassériau (at number 14), the director Jean Renoir (at number 4); or the villa Montmorency, which was the château of the comtesse de Boufflers, who is famous as having been one of the key figures of the 18th century. The Goncourt brothers moved in here in 1868, and created the famous "*Grenier*", the salon where the writers who would make up the first Goncourt Academy would meet. André Gide also had a Cubist house here, which was a leading attraction for young writers at the beginning of the century. Others which also resembled villages in the country were the hameau de Boulainvilliers, where the author Pierre Louÿs lived; the hameau Boileau, which name comes from the country house that was on the same site in the 17th century, and whose famous resident was the sculptor Carpeaux, and the villa Saïd where Anatole France had his intellectual salon.

The Cité Fleurie is more closely linked to artistic life, especially to the memory of the painter Henri Cadiou, and this space is an exceptional bit of nature in an unexpected location, near the Santé prison. There were houses that doubled as workshops, beautiful paths lined with flowers; it was really just like being in the country. One that was more austere was the villa Seurat, which is marked by the cubist architecture designed by André Lurçat, and Auguste Perret who built a studio there for the sculptor Chana Orloff. This also played its role in 20th century cultural life through one of its disruptive inhabitants, Henry Miller, and the painter Mario Prassinos.

Another legendary spot is the Ruche (Beehive), which was similar to the Bateau Lavoir in Montmartre. The sculptor Boucher salvaged what was left of some buildings designed by Eiffel for the 1900 World Exhibition, with the goal of making an artists' phalanstery. His goal was met, with a certain amount of disorder, but also glory that shone on him because of the famous people that lived here, even though sometimes many of them lived there in total misery, such as Chagall, who Blaise Cendrars would visit in the 1910s. There were also many emigrant artists come from Eastern Europe who had studios here, such as Soutine, Kremegne, Kikoine, Zadkine and Archipenko. A new wave of artists moved in here after the Second World War, including Paul Rebeyrolle, and more recently Biras, Simone Dat, André Elbaz, Gastaud, Lucio Fantin and Ernest Pignon-Ernest.

Parisian musicians are becoming rarer in streets that are overwhelmed by modern life. They are part of the city's traditions. They have been wandering the streets for centuries, bearers of a simple familiar form of poetry. It was not long ago that passersby would join in and sing a song together with them, and the musicians would sell the sheet music for these songs for a few sous. This was the time of Édith Piaf, and this was the world she grew up in.

The village Saint-Paul was, during the reign of the first Valois kings (Charles V and his son, the unfortunate mad king), the logis Saint-Pol, a group of houses interconnected by arcades and gardens, which slowly disappeared. But the streets of this quarter still have the same name, as well as an incomparable type of charm that was revived when the buildings here were carefully restored. By connecting the courtyards of the buildings in this quarter, a quaint pedestrian area was created, highlighted by charming shops and flea markets.

Flower markets pop up unexpectedly at intersections (place des Ternes), along the Seine (quai aux Fleurs), and their decoration changes with the rhythm of the seasons. These are the anterooms of love stories, as they were seen in the French cinema of the nineteen thirties.

There are still many small cités, old groups of houses, which manage to maintain a provincial atmosphere against the backdrop of tall buildings, of more intentional architecture. Imagination runs rampant in these tiny gardens, as seen here in the rue de Mouzaïa, in the 19th arrondissement.

Gérard de Nerval spoke of the grape harvest in Montmartre: "There are even grapes, the last ones used to make the famous wine from Montmartre, which competed with those from Argenteuil and Suresnes during Roman times. This humble vineyard looses another row of its shrivelled vines each year, which fall into a quarry... This is where you have the best view of Paris. What I always appreciated in this small space protected by the huge trees of the Château des Brouillards, was this small bit of vineyard which remains, and brings back memories of Saint Denis..."

Grapes are harvested even from the smallest vines, here on rue Léon-Frot, in the 11th arrondissement.

Any reason to celebrate is fine, and especially when wine is the reason. Montmartre is a permanent celebration, animated by sights and sounds which bring back memories of the village that it was when Nerval spoke of its charm: "There are windmills, cabarets and arbors, green paradises and silent streets, running along houses with thatched roofs, barns and thick gardens, green plains where springs flow from the earth…"

Wheat on the Champs-Élysées. One fine summer day, farmers in a festive mood organized a huge public relations operation to give people a closer look at what their work was like. Seeing this strange picture, one can imagine a surrealist collage showing the Opéra in the middle of a prairie surrounded by cows.

The Underbelly of the City

The Parvis de Notre-Dame, the remains of the old Louvre, the Catacombs, the sewers, the metro

Metro stations can also be used to highlight the cultural life of the places it passes beneath. They can be an echo of life above ground. The Varenne metro station stops next to the Rodin museum. One of his sculptures fits in here perfectly.

Like all cities whose origins go back so far, the underground of Paris contains many elements that are remnants of its previous lives. It is almost impossible to dig anywhere in Paris without coming across vestiges of its past. There are many traces of the passages and dwellings of its different inhabitants, and a great deal of archeological activity is constantly underway. Of all the sites that are open and accessible to the public, the most impressive is that of the Parvis de Notre-Dame. This dig has unearthed proof of human activity at this site dating back to the very origins of Lutetia, and throughout the different periods of its existence.

Excavation has also recently occurred around the foundations of the old Louvre, and findings here show the size of the château, when it was strictly defensive, and whose infrastructures determined the fate of the current Louvre. Its thick strong walls can again be seen, in a discreet but efficient presentation, in all their nobility and majesty. This is a rare example of architectural perfection, and this type of example can be found following the path of the city wall that was built by Philip Augustus.

A constant enlargement of the metro network is one of the great adventures of Parisian urbanization. The RER suburban trains take passengers approximately 50 kilometers from the center of Paris, and connect with the metro. The Éole network is used to relieve some of the heavy traffic on the RER. The map of the metro is a guide for travellers hoping to find their way in this modern version of the Labyrinth. But this one has no Minotaur.

While there is this civilized Paris, which was urbanized by human effort, there is also that part of the city that is a result of this urbanization: the hollow underground part of Paris.

A huge network of underground tunnels was created, as a result of the extraction of stone needed to build the city. The quarries of Paris have been the subject of many crazy rumors and legends.

The first quarries date back to the Gallo-Roman period, and it was around the year 1000 that Parisians were building with stones cut from quarries on the left bank, near the château de Vauvert (allée de l'Observatoire), an abandoned country home belonging to Robert le Pieux, inhabited by the fringe of Paris.

As the centuries went by, the network of underground passages kept growing, and was finally put to use when certain Parisian cemeteries, considered dangerous for their surroundings, were moved. The cimetière des Innocents, which was very old, was a source of disease, and had to be removed because of this health hazard. The cemetery was emptied of its bodies in 1786. A number of other cemeteries were progressively emptied: Saint-Eustache, Saint-Étienne-du-Grès, Saint-Landry, Sainte-Croix-de-la-Bretonnerie, Saint-André-des-Arts and the cimetière des Errancis (place Prosper-Coubaux, where many famous people had been buried, such as Madame Élisabeth, Danton, Camille Desmoulins, Robespierre, Hébert, Fabre d'Églantine, Chaumette, Malesherbes and Saint-Just).

The Catacombs, given this name in a reference to those in Rome, became a popular site. Parties were held here and, open to tourists, they show visitors a strange, morbid and sententious sight.

The Père-Lachaise cemetery (here the tomb of Jim Morrison) is one of the strangest Parisian cemeteries, because of the people who lie there as well as the variety, and often quality, of the funerary architecture that can be seen there. It started out, in 1430, as La Folie Regnault, a sort of country house belonging to a rich merchant. The Jesuits purchased this house as a residence for François de la Chaise d'Aix, who was called the père La Chaise (father La Chaise), and who was the the confessor to Louis XIV. This is the origin of the name for this cemetery that was created by Napoléon and built by Brongniart in 1804, who maintained its country-like atmosphere. To give it a certain prestige, it was decided to move the Monument to Abélard and Héloïse, a somewhat excessive Troubadour style monument, that Alexandre Lenoir had built in his Champs Élyséens (today the École des Beaux-Arts). The magnificent monument that closes the view from the main entrance is the work of Bartholomé. This cemetery is an absolute who's who of artists, writers, musicians and thinkers, who have come here to sleep their final sleep. Among the most famous are Géricault, Apollinaire, Marie Joseph Chénier, Bernardin de Saint-Pierre, Benjamin Constant, Cuvier, Nodier, Balzac, Nerval, Chopin, Delacroix, Michelet, Bizet, Claude Bernard, Gustave Doré, Alphonse Daudet, Pissarro, Sarah Bernhardt, Anna de Noailles, Colette, and the strange 32-square tomb that Raymond Roussel had built for himself.

Léon Bopp, in Paris, commented on Napoléon's tomb in the Invalides: "Under this dome, at the bottom of a sort of tank as if it were a wine, a supernatural spirit, perhaps fine Napoléon [a type of cognac]: Napoléon! at the bottom of a sort of ditch, as if we were in the presence of a dangerous clawed animal; Napoléon! at the bottom of a well, as if it were the well of Truth in person. So he lies in that tomb which sent the sculptor Pradier to his own tomb, in this red granite tomb standing on a green granite base, and all that is missing to have the colors of Italy would be a bit of white. Blood red? Almost."

On the parvis of Notre-Dame, "mystery plays" were presented in the Middle Ages. These were shows whose goal was to teach the crowds about the main events of Holy History. The desire for flashy shows led to Biblical stories presented in circus-like conditions, with impressive scenery.

Paris, as a necropolis, was adorned with some of the most surprising settings, where eternal rest mingled with the myth of its gardens, but this part of the city remained linked, by its activity, to the idea of a city with a dark underworld.

The Montmartre cemetery and the Montparnasse cemetery contend for the tombs of the most important figures of the capital's social and cultural life. But it is the Père-Lachaise cemetery which is the most important, because of its size, its country-like atmosphere, the artistic quality of its tombs and the who's who of the deceased that can be seen there. It contains the tombs of the most important figures in all fields of thought and History.

The Panthéon is also a tomb, but a tomb of glory. It was built by Soufflot, in an austere style of architecture, which corresponds to its previous role as a church, and is the temple of a Fatherland honoring the Glories of its great men and women.

Pompously alone, Napoléon's tomb stands in the midst of a circle beneath the dome of the Invalides church; a tomb designed by Visconti, surrounded by twelve victories carved in marble by Pradier. Many famous members of the military are also buried there (Sérusier, Jourdan, Damrémont, Oudinot, Molitor, Mac Mahon, Kléber and d'Ornano), names which are reminders of boulevards and avenues that also honor their great feats.

Paris also has its cloaca maxima: its sewers. For a long time it had no sewers, and was known to be one of the filthiest cities in the western world. The chronicler Sébastien Mercier, who had an eye for detail, noted in the 18th century that "Parisians' eyes and noses are used to filth". The Bièvre River and the Ménilmontant Stream were natural spillways, and became the Great Sewer. In 1605, realizing the risks of epidemics, a project was developed to cover this waterway, but it was not until the reign of Louis XV that work was started. The work that had been completed was only done roughly and there was neither cohesion nor unity in it. Belgrand developed a sewer system covering the entire city, at the very moment when it was absorbing its neighboring towns and breaking itself down into twenty arrondissements.

The different sections of the underground sewers (a sort of city beneath the city, which corresponds more or less to its streets) have an intense power to tap our imagination, and Victor Hugo used this brilliantly in *Les Misérables*, which gives a powerful description of the journey of a modern Dante.

The sewers can be visited in rowboats. The most imaginative visitors may dream of Caron, crossing the Styx. But, at the end of this expedition, there is no hell as promised by the ancient texts. The ultimate use of the underground was the creation of the Métropolitain for the World Exhibition of 1900. Line 1, which goes from Vincennes to Maillot follows the city's historic direction of growth, and stops at some of its main landmarks, such as the Champs-Élysées crossroads, where the buildings of this huge exhibit were built. The work was entrusted to an engineer named Fulgence-Bienvenüe, who is one of the final names in this gallery of talented, resolute men who designed modern Paris. The constant enlargement of the metro network has followed the growth of this city at work. It is one of the main tools in the life of Parisian workers. The slogan shouted during the revolts of May 68, "metro - boulot - dodo" (metro - work - sleep), shows how negatively it was perceived by its daily riders. But for its occasional visitors, its colors, its fervent life and above all its odor are an essential part of their impressions of Paris. It was with a metro ticket in hand that the hero of *The Salary of Fear* died, in that famous film made by Clouzot from the novel by Georges Arnaud.

The Butte Montmartre

Sacré-Cœur, the Moulin de la Galette, the Lapin Agile

Much maligned when it was built, the Sacré-Cœur is today an integral part of the Parisian landscape. This is an emblem for the city, like the Arc de Triomphe de l'Étoile and the Eiffel Tower. Together, these are the three main symbols of Parisian legend. The steps of its gardens, and its terraces, make the climb to the summit more of a relaxing walk than a pious ascent, since Montmartre contains so many stories which help change this area from a peaceful village to a tourist attraction.

In the tradition of street singers who practiced their art in the Middle Ages, these engaging and picturesque characters sing of the charms of Paris.

Montmartre is like a village, with its codes, its customs, and even its own city hall that looks as if it were a parody. For a long time this was a country-like area, and it was progressively integrated into the big city without entirely losing that special something that gives it its own charm, its own personality and its past. Its geographic location made it a perfect spot to put windmills. There were thirteen of them. All that remain are some merry vestiges such as those of the Moulin de la Galette, that was immortalized by Renoir, which was changed into a music hall. This set the tone for the entire Butte (Hill), and when the work went away it became an area devoted to pleasure.

There is nothing left of the Abbey that flourished here for centuries except the names of some of the streets, and the construction of the Sacré-Cœur, which was decided in 1873, which renewed the religious activity of the hill. The huge basilica, finished in 1912, which was highly contested, is now a part of the familiar skyline of Paris, just like the Eiffel tower. Its construction led to the development of its surrounding land as gardens whose successive levels and harmonious combinations highlight the steep slope of the land. The Butte Montmartre had long been hedged farmland, with fields of grain divided by grapevines (there is a tiny vineyard remaining on the rue Saint-Vincent). Steep paths ran through these fields (what are now the rue Ravignan, rue du Mont-Cenis and rue Antoinette) which led to the Saint-Pierre church, the oldest church in Paris (together with Saint-Julien-le-Pauvre). Huge quarries, cathedrals full of shadows, were dug into the ground. These Dantesque spaces were meant for intensive mining of its natural resources.

The stairs that lead up to the Sacré-Cœur have always been a space for children to play, pilgrims to climb and tourists to lose their breath; this is a way to earn the pleasure of going into the cool, dark basilica. Max Jacob, when living on Montmartre and sharing misery with the young Picasso, climbed to the top of the Butte every morning for the early mass. The sinner wanted to punish himself for his escapades of the previous night.

Like a lighthouse standing above the storm, the dome of the Sacré-Cœur dominates the lively activity of the boulevard. This is the setting for some of the shady activities that fascinated Francis Carco and fed his literature: Jésus la Caille, Pigalle…

The pastoral atmosphere of this area attracted a population of artists and bohemians at the beginning of the 20th century while Paris was growing. This new population gave Montmartre its cachet.

The many people who wrote lyrically of this golden age of "Montmartrian Bohemia" (Roland Dorgelès, Francis Carco, André Warnod, Paul Yakia and Pierre Mac Orlan) described most of what made up the legend of this area. Between the Château des Brouillards (where Gérard de Nerval and Renoir lived) and the Bateau-Lavoir (where Picasso and Van Dongen had their studios) is a web of memories where the shadows of Reverdy and Max Jacob, of Suzanne Valadon and Utrillo meet.

Many cafés and small restaurants welcomed this good-natured, inspired, picturesque society. All that remains from that time is the legendary Lapin Agile, the former Cabaret des Assassins, a sort of "fin de siècle" music-hall, frequented by Caran d'Ache, Courteline, Maurice Rollinat, Verlaine, Alphonse Allais, Léon Bloy and Forain, in a fraternity of happy misery and uninhibited joy. With its small shaded terrace, it is the only precious bit of countryside that remains. On top of the hill, at 12 rue Cortot, there is also an old farm, and one of its first inhabitants was Rosimond, an actor in Molière's company. Renoir lived here in 1875, along with Émile Bernard, and the infernal trio of Suzanne Valadon, her husband Utter and her son Utrillo, together with Léon Bloy, the pamphleteer, and Erik Satie, the satiric composer and collaborator of Picasso and Cocteau, on the show Parade, which created a scandal at the Châtelet theater.

At night, the esplanade of Sacré-Cœur gives one of the most famous and cherished views of Paris. The city seems to spread as far as the horizon, and at night, the many glittering lights make up a fascinating landscape. "There is a view over this sea of grey, which is bluish and smoky, with walls, roofs and chimneys; and where here or there some tall buildings stand out, mostly churches, churches with square towers or pointed bell towers or rounded domes, nothing but churches, churches, there must be hundreds."

When in 1886 the Lapin Agile was a music hall, it was frequented by Caran d'Ache, Courteline, Rollinat, Renoir, Alphonse Allais, Verlaine and Léon Bloy. Then came the generation of "Montmartrians" around Picasso, Max Jacob, André Warnod and Roland Dorgelès. The Lapin Agile (also called the Lapin à Gill, after the name of the person who painted its sign), was run by a picturesque person that Pierre Mac Orlan (who married his daughter) made a lively portrait of. He "wore a red scarf tied behind his neck like the fishermen of the South… he wore boots and walked silently, he was nimble, massive and courageous, his back was bent, his head down, he was ready for both attack and defense…"

Albert Mérat, the wonderful poet who wrote Images of Paris, wrote: "On Sundays, they still go up / Following small streets / Up to the Moulin de la Galette." This is the scenery as it was painted by Renoir, and immortalized by his famous painting. A bit of the charm of Montmartre when it was still just a village.

Jules Romains recalled in Lovers' Journey: "You know, when we went to eat dinner / Under the trees at the place du Tertre / Children played, children laughed / That was the world that surrounded us / All we needed to hear then / Was a voice at the end of the square / It was enough even to see / One branch higher than the wall / To realize that this happiness / Had just gone by somewhere / And that if we hurried, maybe / We could catch it again."

The place du Tertre is the heart of Montmartre. All of its streets lead there, and all of its streets leave in lazy winding paths. Painters crowd together there, in a picturesque rivalry to show their prints and paintings, which correspond to a certain idea that people at the other end of the world have of Paris.

The charm of the Butte is now relegated to the past. Léon-Paul Fargue mentioned that "Montmartre exists because it is, for most of our contemporaries, youth. Marie Laurencin, Derain, Mac Orlan, Salmon and so many others who made their best friends "up there" know this well."

The Studios of Montparnasse

La Rotonde, Le Dôme, La Coupole

The Montparnasse Tower was designed by four architects: Baudoin, Cassau, De Hoym de Marien and Saubot. A panoramic viewpoint was created on the roof, as well as a panoramic restaurant.

Each generation adopts its own neighborhood, and the cultural history of Paris presents a series of places (sometimes just an intersection, or just one address) where the cultural life of a given period took form. After the Bohemian period of the Butte Montmartre, which lost popularity after the First World War, Montparnasse took over. One simple intersection (Raspail), with two cafés on its corners (Le Dôme and la Rotonde), saw successive waves of artists fleeing their countries and finding political and economic refuge in Paris, as well as a public for their work. There was no structure to this adventure, only a friendliness which challenged institutions but did not prevent misery. At this time, Montparnasse was still on the outskirts of the active heart of the capital.

At the top of the "boul'mich" (boulevard Saint-Michel), praised by Francis Carco, is the Closerie des Lilas. This café was popular with the Symbolist poets and served as a link between literary and artistic activities. Together with Paul Fort, the "prince of Poets", the editors of the many little magazines which flourished at the beginning of the century, and were tribunes for new ideas and new talents, would gather. Guillaume Apollinaire, André Salmon and André Rouveyre honored them with their contributions.

There were many artists who came from Eastern Europe (Soutine, Krémègne, Kikoine, Chagall, Archipenko, Brancusi, Zadkine, Pascin), but Montparnasse was such an attraction that the entire country would soon be represented there (Modigliani, Picasso, Miró, Dali, Brauner, Hérold, Dominguez, Torrès-Garcias, Kisling and Foujita).

These people often spoke very poor French, but they managed to become an integral part of this neighborhood that they were helping to change, mobilizing some spaces, making some addresses famous (rue Campagne-Première, rue Falguière) and establishing this quarter among a unity of creative energy where poets served as translators and introduced new authors, using their enthusiasm to help popularize new creations. Cendrars and Cocteau were instrumental in the progressive recognition of the artists of Montparnasse.

Nightlife here was lively and friendly, and this is what the photographer Brassaï managed to capture in his pictures, which remain some of the best records of Paris during the Roaring Twenties.

The Montparnasse Tower was built from 1969 to 1973 at the same time as the neighboring train station was totally renovated, which led to major changes in the surrounding area. Fifty-six of its fifty-nine floors are used for offices, and it is more than two hundred meters high.

The Bright Lights of Pigalle

The Élysée-Montmartre, the Moulin Rouge, and the cabarets of today and yesterday

The Moulin-Rouge is a theater for night owls, and its bright lights express its meaning and beauty. It has become a part of the legend of Gay Paris, since a few famous "variety show" artists (La Goulue, Valentin le Désossé) were painted by the lively, truculent hand of Toulouse-Lautrec, who was a regular there. He considered them the vital subjects for his work as an artist.

Parallel to the Grands Boulevards, which run from the place de la République to the place de la Madeleine, and which have created one of the features of the capital, the street which runs from the Barbès-Rochechouart crossroads to place Clichy changed many times over the years. It has since become the avenue which best represents modern sexuality, in its most common visual aspect, with sexy window displays, sex-shops, cheap erotic shows and the shady characters that these elements attract. In this, it is similar to the old rue Saint-Denis, which is now a pedestrian street, and which has also been taken over by a similar influence of the sex entertainment industry.

In the 19th century, this was a place where people came for innocent festivity; it was then populated by artists, whose studios were scattered all along this road, contributing to an exciting atmosphere. Such artists as Toulouse-Lautrec, Degas, Seurat and Pascin lived here, while Francis Carco wrote with fascination about the women of the night and their protectors. These people were the sources for his literature which was both colorful and sophisticated, picturesque and cruel, and which described the singular nature of this boulevard which was often painted by the artists of the 19th century, such as Van Gogh. This boulevard has only changed slightly since then; fairground stalls now often occupy the island in the middle of the avenue. The facades of the buildings, which were once apartments for the bourgeoisie, are now little more than ground floor window displays with bright colors and mirrors, inviting the crowds of passersby, overwhelmed by many such indecent propositions, to come in and watch one of the non-stop shows.

Along this colorful and provocative road, some of the energy that was here during the 19th century when Toulouse-Lautrec was a familiar face to the people of this neighborhood, and when he decorated the La Goulue stall, still remains.

Almost side by side on the boulevard de Rochechouart, stand theaters that have lost the prestige they once had, such as the Élysée Montmartre at number 72, which was a popular ballroom when opened (in 1807) and which inherited decorations from the Bal Mabille. Its neighbor, the Trianon, was a theater for operettas at the beginning of the century, and was then used for a variety of purposes which altered its old-fashioned charm. Nothing is left from the movie theater at number 120, which was the Bal de la Boule Noire, founded in 1822 by a woman of easy virtue, and which had a dubious reputation. This is where the Quadrille des Lanciers was created. The theater which took its place was named La Cigale, and is currently used as a

A wild neon sign shining in the Parisian night sky. Blaise Cendrars and Apollinaire praised the modernity of these signs.

concert hall. The boulevard de Clichy is next to it. Many theaters whose names have gone down in history existed during the 19th century: the Taverne du Bagne (at number 2), the bal de l'Ermitage (at number 6) in the building where Degas died in 1917, the Cabaret du Néant (at number 34), La Lune Rousse (at number 36), the cabaret des Quat'z-Arts where the poet Jehan Rictus held sway (at number 62), Le Tambourin (at number 64), where Van Gogh exposed his paintings, le caveau du Chat Noir (at number 68), which is similar to a place that Rodolphe Salis ran on the boulevard de Rochechouart, and which was frequented by Aristide Bruant, and finally, at number 100, the théâtre des Deux-nes which was a cabaret. This boulevard goes from the place Pigalle to the place Blanche and ends up at the place Clichy.

In the 19th century, the place Pigalle was the site of a model market. While waiting to be hired, the painters' models would wait along the edge of the pool in the center of the square.

There, in an atmosphere of permanent excitement that even the night could not attenuate, were the famous Abbaye de Thélème (at number 1), the cabaret du Rat Mort (at number 7) which was frequented by Gambetta, Jules Vallès, Henri Rochefort, Courbet, Manet and François Coppée, the Nouvelle Athens (at number 9), which was the meeting place for the Impressionists from 1870 on. Seedy strip-tease joints later took their place.

At the end of rue Blanche is the square that gives this street its name, place Blanche, which is best known for having been a meeting place for the Surrealists. André Breton, their mentor, lived nearby at 42 rue Fontaine. The Moulin Rouge was also here, spreading its wings. This was the breeding ground for young dandies who would come here slumming and admire the choreographic skills of "boneless" Valentin, La Goulue, Grille d'Égout, and Nini Patte en l'Air, a pathetic crowd that Toulouse-Lautrec immortalized, showing the attitudes and tragic fates behind the glitter. Boris Vian, the poet and novelist, lived on the terrace overlooking the square, and Jacques Prévert was a neighbor.

Place Clichy had a strategic location in Paris when the boundaries of the city ended there. During Napoléon's last French campaign, in 1814, it was the site of a final heroic defense led by Marshal Moncey (his statue stands today in the center of the square), whose headquarters were in the Père Lathuille restaurant (avenue de Clichy), made famous in a painting by Manet. It was at the Clichy gate that Louis XVIII got into "the trunks of the enemy in 1815", and ran away from Paris, during the turbulent period of the One Hundred Days.

Train Stations

The gare Saint-Lazare and Impressionism, the Orsay Museum

A bell tower, 64 meters high, with clocks on all four sides, was added to the gare de Lyon, which had been built by the architect Denis Tardoire in 1899. This bell tower reinforces the majestic character of the train station.

The construction of the first train stations in Paris took place during a time of great changes in the 19th century, and completed baron Haussmann's Parisian urbanization projects. The opulence of their facades, which did not correspond to their function, was a continuation of the habit of making public buildings look rich to give them greater importance in daily life. But these buildings met very specific needs, and were among the first to take advantage of major advances in architecture, by using iron girders and glass to harmoniously develop their spaces.

There are six train stations in Paris, each of them leading to a different part of France - the railways like so many blood vessels maintaining communication between the heart and the rest of the body.

The gare du Nord has trains leaving for England, Belgium, the Netherlands and Scandinavia; the gare de l'Est has trains that go through the Germanic countries to the far horizons of Eastern Europe; the gare de Lyon, wears the colors of Italy that it leads to, as well as the Mediterranean, after having gone through most of the center of France; the gare d'Austerlitz, which goes to the South-West and the beaches along the Atlantic Ocean; the gare Montparnasse which brought many maids to Paris from the far-off countryside of Brittany, and crossed this Western part of France which was still a wild province; and finally the gare Saint-Lazare, the gate to Normandy, which gave the Impressionnists an impulsion and desire to travel. From this station, the luxurious western suburb of Versailles was now nearby, and it also had some smaller trains, like the internal line that went to the porte d'Auteuil and which was long the last vestige of a Parisian railway network.

The "petite ceinture" (small belt) no longer exists; this railway line which surrounded Paris and whose tracks ran along in a deep trench, was a sort of pastoral gash in a Paris that was still growing. All that remains of this line are a few forgotten stations, threatened with extinction, that are visited now only by wandering cats, and that fascinate photographers looking for picturesque sites.

A "suburban network" was connected to the more distant lines, and these trains are used for the daily comings and goings of hard-working sleepy crowds in a hurry, who are the blood of working Paris. Parts of this network have since disappeared, and the most delightful line, which left from a station which was called the gare de la Bastille, has been replaced by a "greenway", which serves as an alibi for huge renovation and gentrification projects. Its rails have been replaced by flagstone paths, in the middle of grass and wild flowers, which wander along atop an ancient viaduct, whose arches contain shops which are becoming increasingly fashionable.

Another survivor, but which is now used as a "station" to take airline passengers to the airports by bus, is the gare des Invalides, which was built by Lisch for the 1900 World Exhibition. It brought visitors from Versailles and the western suburbs to the very heart of this exhibition.

The gare de Sceaux was built at the location of the café François Ier, which was frequented by Verlaine and the Symbolist poets, and this was the terminus for a train line which meandered gently through the wooded hills of the vallée de Chevreuse, and that stopped at towns with delightful names along its route. Its modernization has not affected its delightful routes, but has actually made them more accessible. Paris can breathe better with these relaxing arteries that keep it anchored in a certain idea of country living, which it cultivates even in its gardens and parks.

The oldest train station in Paris is the gare d'Austerlitz. It was built in 1839, as the terminus of a train line heading to Orléans. In 1900, taking advantage of the World Exhibition, its line was lengthened, running it deep into the city to the central, most noble part of the Seine. This would become the gare d'Orsay, which was recently transformed into a museum of the same name.

The gare Saint-Lazare was built in 1840 to be the terminus of an even older railway line, built in 1837, which went to Saint-Germain-en-Laye. Originally, the station was called the Embarcadère de Saint-Germain (the Saint-Germain "pier"). It quickly became too small, and was entirely rebuilt from 1885 to 1889. It was this new version that was painted by Monet.

The Embarcadère du Nord connected Paris to Belgium. It thrilled those who appreciated modernity, and who listened to the voice of Baudelaire. Théophile Gautier, very enthusiastic as usual, wrote: "Tremendous arches, huge roofs, strong buttresses, all these things give this palace of modern industry a distinctive character, a sort of majesty which strikes even the most rebellious. It may be strange that architecture, whose decadence and death have been proclaimed for such a long time, may find that railway stations hold the key to its revival." In 1864, its beautiful facade, by Hittorff, made it look like a palace. It was decorated with huge statues personifying the cities that could be reached with its trains: London, Vienna, Berlin, Brussels and Amsterdam, perpetuating the cultural habits which use mythology, the mother of all our dreams, to present these cities as women who belong to a new era of industry.

The Embarcadère de Strasbourg, inaugurated in 1849, became the gare de l'Est, which was enlarged in 1854, and then again in 1900. It stands, impressively, this space full of painful memories for those soldiers who left here to fight the two world wars, at the end of one of the longest views of the capital, and it can be seen from the place du Châtelet. It looks as if it were a sort of a temple, at the end of the boulevard de Sébastopol and the boulevard de Strasbourg which cut across Paris in what had been one of its medieval areas, which was always full of workers, and roguish in many parts. Its facade, wider than that of the gare du Nord (its neighbor), has a beautiful central arch, which is also dominated by a statue. This station is the work of Duquesney, but it was enlarged in the 1930s.

When the gare de Lyon grew, it brought about the disappearance of the marvelous château de Bercy designed by Le Vau. This enlargement was part of a huge urbanization plan for this part of Paris, which saw the simultaneous creation of both these railways and the Bercy Warehouses. These warehouses perpetuated a tradition dating back to the 18th century, when wine, whose sale was regulated and taxed, was delivered in this same area by boat. The massacre of this area was completed when the Thiers Fortifications, Paris' final city wall, was built.

An imposing clock tower was added to the building by Denis Tardoire in 1900. The interior is a dazzling exercise in rococo decoration with the famous Buffet du Train Bleu (Blue Train Restaurant) decorated by a series of 45 panels which present different cities in France. Together with the Hôtel de Ville, this is one of the most perfect examples of this taste for luxury perpetuated by academic art, full of pastiches and historic references.

Before becoming the museum of 19th century art that it is today, Orsay was the terminus for trains going to Orléans. The station, built by Victor Laloux, was built expressly to take travellers from the gare d'Austerlitz to the World Exhibition of 1900 which was built along the Seine, on the esplanade des Invalides, the Champ de Mars, and the Chaillot hill.

Near what had been the Folie-Boutin, the first Tivoli, one of the essential places to be seen during the Directoire, famous for its picturesque gardens where even Marie-Antoinette would not hesitate to join the crowd, the gare Saint-Lazare, which was built as the terminus for the first railway, was inaugurated in great pomp in 1837. It was renovated in 1889-90, to take on its current appearance. The place de l'Europe, built on a metallic structure, covers the inextricable network of rails that leave from this station and which shakes the entire rue de Rome. This square was one of the favorite settings for the painter Caillebotte.

The architect Victor Lenoir handled the construction of the gare Montparnasse in 1852. It quickly became too small, and was enlarged with great difficulty in the small space available within the rectangle formed by the rue du Départ, rue de l'Arrivée, place de Rennes and avenue du Maine, before undergoing a final and more radical transformation in 1958, when the entire quarter was renovated.

The Orsay Museum is "lodged" in the concourse of the old station, maintaining as much as possible of what makes this a typical example of late 19th century architecture.

This restaurant was the interior of a luxurious hôtel that was included in the train station. Now as a museum, it has conserved the precious setting for its dining rooms, salons and galleries, which correspond to the heavy, luxurious "fin de siècle" style.

Shopping Arcades

The galerie Vivienne, the passage des Panoramas, the passage Colbert

In the heart of the boulevards and their dense traffic, at the center of Paris, near the lively Bourse, the many arcades are a haven of silence and calm (here the passage des Panoramas). Never overcrowded, they contained a strange, often murky light, that Aragon, in The Night-Walker, *compared to that of an aquarium.*

While arcades are not exclusively Parisian, they are one element of the city that give it its own special character. Almost all Parisian arcades were built in the 19th century. The 18th century saw a precursor of this idea, with the arcades in the Palais Royal. They are intimate spaces for people to shop and meet, and most of them were developed on the right bank, near the Grands Boulevards, where they act as a confidential and sometimes clandestine continuation. Unusual shops were set up here, luxurious spaces selling often luxury goods, and brothels. Aragon, in *The Night-Walker*, pointed out the strange quality of life that was found in these arcades, and suggested that they were like aquariums, where the appearance and even the behavior of those who came to the arcades was different than when out in open air.

From the rue du Faubourg-Montmartre to the rue Saint-Marc, there is a clear passage that goes through a number of blocks and crosses streets, creating a very unusual series of arcades with antique shops, used book stores and tea rooms (these arcades are called the passage Verdeau, passage Jouffroy, and passage des Panoramas). The major attraction of this area is the musée Grévin and its wax figures, which present some of the main characters in French History, in naive but historically correct tableaux. Near the Bibliothèque Nationale, the passage Vivienne and the passage Colbert have been recently restored and renovated. Near the avenue de l'Opéra, and opening on to the théâtre des Bouffes Parisiens, the passage Choiseul has managed to retain something of its past, even though the publisher Alphonse Lemerre, attached to the

Near the Bibliothèque Nationale, and next to the rue Vivienne which is at the heart of the night-time wanderings of Lautréamont's Maldoror (he was then living in 15 rue Vivienne), the galerie Vivienne, which has recently been restored, was a place where it was easy to forget the world and remember a time when Paris was more intimate. However, it was here in the 19th century that the legendary Vidocq lived, that the famous Petit Théâtre de Marionnettes (Little Puppet Theater) attracted theater goers, and also here that exhibits of "Incoherent Art" were held, which were a foretaste of Dadaism.

movement of the Parnassiens (Sully Prudhomme, Leconte de Lisle...) and the strange career of Raymond Roussel, is no longer there. The passage Choiseul inspired Céline who described this in *Journey to the End of the Night*. Going up to the carrefour Richelieu-Drouot, there is another arcade that was saved from destruction, the passage des Princes. The passage de l'Opéra was not as lucky, but it has survived in the pages of literature, and has become a place of legend because it was the meeting place for the Dadaist poets, who later went on to create Surrealism.

There are some smaller, less luxurious arcades along the boulevard de Sébastopol and the boulevard de Strasbourg (passage Bourg-l'Abbé, passage Saint-Denis, passage Ponceau, passage Prado, passage Brady) which continue into the small neighboring streets (rue du Grand-Cerf, rue du Caire), now occupied by the vibrant wholesale garment business of the Sentier quarter.

A bit off the beaten path, the passage Véro-Dodat is one of the most beautifully decorated arcades. Straight and luxuriously decorated by "uniform shops, with windows of clear glass held together by copper bars burnished to look like gold, with doors also made of glass, topped by a beautiful decoration of gilded rosettes and palm leaves, and the floor paved in marble", according to the enthusiastic description made in 1837 by the writer of a guide. Some of its former luxury still remains, and the shops which are there fit perfectly into this vestige of magnificence.

It is significant that when examining Paris as a space and object with a constantly evolving social vision, Walter Benjamin studied the geography of these arcades, giving the capital, through the analysis of these spaces, a more dreamlike description than an historic one. Carried away by the object that incarnated its subject, he transcended reality to invent a space that resembled that of the great legendary myths. This is a theatrical area with a universal scope.

Page 216:
The passage Brady was originally a link between the rue du Faubourg-Saint-Denis and the rue Faubourg-Saint-Martin, before the boulevard de Strasbourg was built. Opened in 1828, it contained a hundred stores and huge spaces available for industry. The magazine Le Moniteur Universel, *which criticized it, specified that it was merely "a bazaar for used clothes and nothing else; there are many merchants and many reading rooms" as well as a bathing house. It never awakened from its long sleep.*

Page 217:
The galerie Véro-Dodat owes its name to two pork butchers who financed it in 1826. Among the stores that were set up here, there was an art dealer who sold etchings, and particularly caricatures by Charivari. He sold works signed Gavarni, Daumier and Henri Monnier. The actress Rachel lived in the building visited by Alfred de Musset, who wrote a story called Supper with Mademoiselle Rachel. *This arcade has been very nicely restored, and there are nice shops, including the famous doll specialist Robert Capia.*

Water in the City

The Arsenal basin, the canal Saint-Martin, the fountains of Paris

At the foot of the palais de Chaillot, built for the World Exhibition of 1937, is a park with a huge pool and powerful fountains with water effects. There is a group of sculptures representative of the state of this art during the Roaring Twenties, which is caught between the boldness of Modernism, but which still bears the mark of classicism.

Wallace fountains, spread out around Paris, were the gift of a rich English art collector who had thought of giving his collections, which contained works of 18th century French art, to Paris. Seeing the shortcomings of a government who seemed to spurn the prestigious gift he wished to make, Wallace decided to move his collections to London. An important museum there is dedicated to them. The fountains, which are made for the masses, were supposed to console Paris for the loss of those masterpieces of its past.

Here in Paris, like everywhere else, water was worshipped. Roman wisdom overcame the fantasy of sources sprouting up just anywhere and wandering to other sites. First water was shared, then it was distributed, and then requested. As Paris got bigger, it needed more and more of this precious water, and water supply systems were built to bring it to the city. There are still some parts remaining of the one built by Marie de Médicis to bring water to her Luxembourg Palace.

There were also thoughts of bringing water from the Marne and Ourcq rivers, but the projects, which were studied seriously, were not developed. It was not until Napoléon that this work was carried out. At the same time, he decided that he wanted to build "eighty-four fountains that flow day and night throughout the summer". A series of fountains would be built and decorated with sculptures. Some of these still remain: the fontaine de La Paix (allée du Séminaire), the fontaine de Mars (129 rue Saint-Dominique) and the fontaine de l'Égyptien (rue de Sèvres), with a statue inspired by an Egyptian sculpture in the Capitole Museum.

These fountains were built in the styles of the time: Neoclassical, Egyptian, Greek or Roman. These were virile and patriotic edifices. This was a way of leaving a mark, but which never competed with the incomparable grace of the fontaine des Innocents, with its gracefully carved nymphs by Jean Goujon.

Some of these fountains can still be seen in today's Paris, and they show that the problem of water is a permanent one.

The fontaine des Innocents, designed by Jean Goujon, was originally a loggia with three arches up against the wall of the Saints-Innocents church, which is no longer in existence. Saved from destruction, the three nymphs sculpted by Goujon were placed on a structure with four walls. Augustin Pajou added the missing figure. For a long time, this fountain was in the middle of a neighborhood square, and was replaced when the Halles quarter was renovated, and raised from the ground to highlight its excellence without cutting it off from the life of the neighborhood inhabitants. It fits in harmoniously with its surroundings.

Built by Visconti in 1847, the fontaine Saint-Sulpice contains statues of four great French churchmen: Bossuet, Fénelon, Massillon and Fléchier. François Derre added the lions that lay at the four corners of the fountain, holding the coat of arms of the city between their paws.

One of the particularities of this water distribution system, which often dates back to ancient times, is that many of these fountains are now surrounded by more recent monuments; this is proof that there has been constant attention made to ensure that the population has access to water.

The hôtel de Soissons, built by Bullant under orders from Catherine de Médicis who was leaving the Tuileries, covered an area which is today partly taken up by the Bourse du Commerce (the old stock market) which has replaced the Halle au Blé (Wheat market). A famous column still stands, and the queen would not hesitate to climb to its summit with her astrologers. When the hôtel de Soissons disappeared completely, after various reincarnations replaced it, the column, which was miraculously preserved, was converted into a fountain in 1812.

The fountain called the fontaine de Médicis, built in 1620 by Salomon de Brosse, in the Luxembourg garden, and moved when the rue de Médicis was constructed, saw the addition of a water spout to its back, bringing water from the rue du Regard, and is decorated with a delicate bas relief of *Leda and the Swan*.

Another beautiful fountain is the fontaine Louis-le-Grand, which was designed from sketches by Jean Beausire in 1707. It is now called the fontaine Gaillon, named after the square where it is located. It was entirely redesigned in 1827 by Visconti.

The fountain designed to bring water to the noble quarter of Saint-Germain was decorated with sculptures by Bouchardon in 1739. It is set in an attractive curve at 57-59 rue de Grenelle.

François I had a pavilion built in 1529 by François Miron. This was called the pavillon de la Croix du Trahoir, at the center of the carrefour de l'Arbre-Sec. It was moved and entirely rebuilt by Soufflot in 1775, and this rebuilt version can be seen today.

The most famous of all Parisian fountains is the fountain in Châtelet called the fontaine de la Victoire, also called the fontaine du Palmier. It was built in 1806, with sculptures by Boizot, and it was moved in 1858 to be across from the pont au Change. Originally, this water outlet adjoined the Grand-Châtelet wall.

The fountain on the place Saint-Sulpice was built by Visconti. This was part of a major urbanization project, to build around the square, which was never completed; a model of what this was to look like can be seen in the building (at number 6). Standing above a pool framed

This pool, above the "bunker" of the IRCAM (Institute for Acoustic and Musical Research), is located between the Centre Pompidou and the Saint-Merri church. It contains a playful farcical fountain. It was designed by the artists Tinguely and Niki de Saint-Phalle. Their judicious work associates the shaky mobility of Tinguely's animated sculptures and the grotesquely unusual gallery of Niki de Saint-Phalle's monsters. This wonderful combination adds humor to the water that seems to dance in a permanent ballet.
To the left, a fountain at the Palais-Royal.

The pont des Arts. In the quivering notes of Meeting with Paris, *Gérard Bauër wrote: "This area is really one of the noble places of the world. Notre-Dame appears at the horizon, standing over the twin towers of the place Dauphine and the square du Vert-Galant which blooms again in every spring just like the youth of King Henri; the most light-hearted of all the wise men among the wise."*

by four lions at rest, is a small structure with four alcoves containing statues of famous churchmen (Bossuet, Fénelon, Massillon and Fléchier).

Another fountain called the fontaine du Château d'Eau was moved from the place de la République (at the time when it was just a large crossroads where the boulevard Saint-Martin, the boulevard du Temple, the rue du Temple and the rue du Faubourg-du-Temple met), and is now at the courtyard of the former La Villette slaughterhouse, which is now the City of Science and Industry. This fountain has three concentric tiered circles, surrounded by eight lions at rest.

Among these many fountains, the most modest ones are those that are often attached to houses. They are better integrated into the surroundings, and sometimes you can walk by and not even notice them, such as the fontaine Palatine (rue Garancière) whose name comes from the princess who paid for it. Another, at the corner of the rue Saint-Denis and the rue Grénéta, is the fontaine de la Reine, or fontaine Grénéta, which was first constructed a very long time ago, in 1400. Rebuilt by François Miron, and again in the 17th century, it hugs the elegant corner of the building that it decorates with style.

There is another fountain located at the corner of two streets (rue des Archives and rue des Haudriettes) which was built in 1624, and was then called the Fontaine Neuve (New Fountain). It was rebuilt in 1770, according to plans by Moreau.

There are other fountains at the corners of the rue Mouffetard and the rue du Pot-de-fer (fontaine Pot de Fer), the rue des Francs-Bourgeois and the rue du Chaume (fontaine de Soubise), the rue Saint-Martin and the rue du Vertbois (fontaine Vertbois).

There is a fountain that is even more discreet, in the impasse de la Poissonnerie, called the fontaine de Jarente, which dates back to the 18th century, and which was renovated in 1783 by M. Carron. The fontaine Maubuée, at the corner of rue Saint-Martin and rue de Venise (opposite the Centre Beaubourg), was built in 1320, and bears witness to that period. It was also entirely rebuilt in 1733.

Some other larger fountains are part of the street decorations. At 184 Faubourg Saint-Antoine is the fontaine de la Petite-Halle, and at 68 rue de la Roquette is the fontaine de la Roquette.

The fontaine Cuvier, formerly called the fontaine de Saint-Victor, dates back to 1806 in its current version. Like other monumental fountains it is majestic. Another such fountain is called the fontaine de Saint-Michel, which is a meeting place for students, and another is the no less famous fontaine Molière, made by Visconti, with sculptures by Pradier. This fountain is at the halfway point on the rue de Richelieu, which is so full of historic memories; on the small square across from the fountain (at number 39) stands the building where Diderot died in 1784. Jeanne Antoinette Poisson, who is almost his contemporary (died in 1764), and is better known under the name Marquise de Pompadour, was born in the beginning of the century at number 50 of the same street. Molière died at number 40 (in 1673) just after having presented his play *The Imaginary Invalid*. This street is full of hôtels and apartments, most of which date back to the 17th and 18th centuries, where they played a key part in the cultural life of that time.

This is Paris' most recent fountain, which is an aquatic response to the transparent rigor of the Pyramid, as if adding movement to accompany its structure, which serves perfectly to highlight the new expansion of the palais du Louvre.

Page 228:
A fountain in the Luxembourg garden. The splendor of water displays is a very important element in the decoration of princely gardens. These fountains, decorated with legendary figures, pour large amounts of water into wide pools laid out along the garden's paths. The Luxembourg garden has all the slightly solemn beauty of royal parks, and the improvised charm that comes from the children who play there. This is the garden of first loves and of poets. Some of these poets even stand as statues along its paths.

The last of the large Parisian parks, the Citroën park takes its name from the site of the Citroën automobile factory, which was at the same location until just after the end of the Second World War. It was designed more to have a pleasant atmosphere that can be enjoyed by its visitors, than to be showy, or to have the intimate charm of pastoral woods.

Page 229:
When the place de la Concorde was enlarged, the two fountains around the Obelisk of Luxor added the fantasy of spouting water to this vast open space. These fountains give aquatic shows.

In his admirable yet familiar walk through his quarter, Léon-Paul Fargue wrote in The Parisian Pedestrian: "It is nice to be able to see calm water, like a jade soup with boats cooking on its surface, with footbridges curved like insects in love, sturdy and desperate quays..." He was thinking of the Saint-Martin canal.

A flea market along the Saint-Martin canal. A growing interest for improvised flea markets goes hand in hand with the evolution of contemporary art, which gives a new poetic mission to a simple choice of manufactured objects. This brings back the past, and is highly critical of our consumer society. Contemporary art maintains relationships through the "leftovers" and waste of daily life, which are as varied as they are intense. Today's flea market is a laboratory for a type of art that listens to our time.

This is where the Arsenal basin, the beginning of the moat that surrounded the Bastille, connects to the Seine. When the Saint-Martin canal was built, its role was changed. Today it is more than just a waterway, but also a village of boats.

Near the La Villette basin, the drawbridge of the rue de Crimée. This was used as a setting for a film by Marcel Carné, based on a novel by Simenon, called Hôtel du Nord. The slow passage of barges through Paris gave this film the poetic feeling of a living city.

Around the new City of Sciences and Industry, a large garden was built along the Ourcq canal. Napoléon had wanted this canal built to bring water to Paris, and today it is used by ships that are sometimes functional but often for tourists, and this adds an unusual note to this area that has adapted to its new role so well.

Gustave Eiffel and his Tower

Utopian dreams

"The Eiffel Tower glows no more. It has become totally serious. It types, day and night, on a typewriter, but sometimes, following a strange order, lights suddenly and covers itself with cold crystal…" said Léon-Paul Fargue in The Parisian Pedestrian.

The engineer Gustave Eiffel is one of the heroes of the adventure of modernism that marked the second half of the 19th century. He believed firmly in progress, and he had a desire to take control of matter and physical phenomena, and to contribute to social betterment, a desire that he shared with these ambitious builders, architects, scientists and doctors who left their mark on the history of the "fin de siècle", even though this history was moving head-on toward an abyss.

The building of this tower, selected as the symbol of the World Exhibition of 1889, gave him a chance to use his utopian genius and technical wisdom to its maximum.

The tower was very controversial; petitions were signed by the leading thinkers of its period (Gounod, Garnier, Victorien Sardou, the son of Alexandre Dumas, François Coppée, Leconte de Lisle, Sully Prudhomme and Guy de Maupassant). But the Eiffel tower won out in the end, and the crowds loved it. Its permanent success has shown that Gustave Eiffel, who made the tower the beacon of his thought, was not mistaken.

For Léon Bloy, Paris "is threatened by this terribly tragic lightpost" and Paul Verlaine, who refused to walk anywhere where he could see it, claims that "this skeleton of a bell tower will not survive", but for Mallarmé it was "beyond his expectations".

Blaise Cendrars celebrated it: "You shine with all the magnificence of the aurora borealis of wireless telegraphy"; in the same vein, Pierre Mac Orlan remarked: "This was Paris, with its tall tower where, every night, the blue hair of the radio crackled, and its parks left the mark of chemical matches on the wall of the night." But the most famous praise of this iron lady, and justly so, is that of Guillaume Apollinaire: "At the end you are weary of this ancient world / Sheperdess Oh Eiffel tower the herd of bridges bleats this morning / You have had enough of living in Greek and Roman antiquity / Here even the automobiles look ancient."

The Eiffel tower is now a part of everyone's world - it has inspired songs, novels and plays, including a play by Jean Cocteau justly entitled *The Newlyweds of the Eiffel Tower*, where Paris was seen from a "bird's eye view".

Painters have also adopted this symbol. From the Douanier Rousseau, who included it in a complacent self-portrait, to Robert Delaunay who fiddled with it with vindictive enthusiasm, to have it flow around broken, excited, jerky rhythm; expressive dislocations of modernism as a factor in a new way of looking at reality. This essential symbol for artists and poets has never lost any of its vitality or its originality.

The Eiffel Tower, according to Pierre Mac Orlan,: "As beautiful for us as the Parthenon was for the Greeks, because it is simple bold lines show the nascent ideas of a new vividness, that we are slowly learning to appreciate and then to love… Passing in front of the tower, the waters of the Seine get young again. This is a great, young, powerful river that dominates the highest tower in the world…"

In this wonderful view of the Champ de Mars, the Eiffel Tower fits in perfectly. This is an expression of urban energy, of modernism, in an area steeped in memory. Wasn't it here, in this exact spot, that the Festival of Federation took place in 1790, which marked the fraternity of all citizens before the French Revolution was plunged into the Terror?

*Page 238:
Far from imposing its presence, the Eiffel Tower blends into a soft melancholic atmosphere that looks as if it comes right out of a poem by Verlaine*

*Page 239:
Even before the painters and sculptors of the 20th century adopted this as a symbol, the Eiffel tower represented the energy of its matter in tense and regular rhythms. These rhythms later inspired the Italian futurists, the first Abstract painters, and can be seen almost identically in the painting of Fernand Léger.*

Worth and Company

The Opéra quarter, the rue de la Paix and the avenue Montaigne

The popularity of department stores (here La Samaritaine) began with the commercial vitality of the Second Empire. They are all marked by an attention to women, whose triumph they celebrate. Fashion results from the same dynamic.

Charles Worth was one of the key figures of the Second Empire. He gave it its style, expressed its frilly luxury, and his reign lasted until the end of the 19th century. Thanks to him, Paris became a capital of fashion, and would remain that way. This is embodied in some of the main figures that have become legendary: Jacques Doucet who was also known as one of the great patrons of the arts of this time, Madeleine Vionnet who made clothes for Lavallière and Cécile Sorel, Paul Poiret who revolutionized fashion by using bright colors; Paquin, Schiaparelli, Nina Ricci, Jeanne Lanvin, Molyneux and especially "Coco" Chanel, whose cold imperious face, praised by Colette, left its mark on the inter-war period of Paris, along with Hermès.

The fashion business, since it was part of the luxury goods trade, was first concentrated around the place Vendôme and the rue de la Paix, and then went further toward the avenue Montaigne, before spreading out across the city as the number of designers increased. This interpenetration of fashion and daily life is a phenomenon that is specific to Paris. The world of art (painting, dance and music) is strongly attached to fashion, and the relationships between art and fashion are beneficial for all, because of the amount of money that flows between them, and the exposure to an international clientele.

Far from trying to drive each other away, the number of fashion designers is constantly increasing. Chanel and many others (Dior, Yves Saint Laurent, Pierre Cardin) are still around while new designers are making their mark: Jean-Paul Gaultier, Daniel Hechter and Christian Lacroix. They all add to the prestige of Paris, giving this city part of what makes it so original and fascinating.

Les Galeries Lafayette. Department stores, a 19th century invention - that Zola called "Le Bonheur des dames" (Women's paradises) - inspired the architecture which designed luxurious cathedrals for them.

The use of new techniques for public buildings of the 19th century made it possible to create huge glass buildings, which were naves of light. These are the many show rooms, the Grand Palais, or the department stores (above the Printemps Haussmann store) which were built throughout Paris.

Pages 248 and 249: Around the avenue Montaigne (formerly the allée des Veuves), are some of the most famous fashion designers of our time, such as Guy Laroche, Nina Ricci and Christian Dior.

The Tastes of Paris

Le Grand Véfour, Lapérouse, La Tour d'Argent, Maxim's

In a courtyard of the Hôtel Crillon.

In the medieval tradition, decorated signs stand outside of restaurants. This was a kind of street art that goes together with the pleasures of the table.

The taste for good food dates back to the distant past, and has long been appreciated and cultivated in Parisian society. Under the Ancien Régime, this was limited to caterers who would deliver selected dishes to people's homes, and lay them out on a table installed according to the whims of the consumers. Dining rooms did not yet exist; they were an invention of the bourgeoisie. And it was the Parisian bourgeoisie that would amplify this phenomenon in restaurants. The late 19th century is full of stories telling of feasts held in restaurants that were the setting for memorable dinners. During the Romantic period this phenomenon increased. The Romantics would eat at the Rocher de Cancale, 59 rue Montorgueil and later 2 rue Mandar, where Balzac and Alexandre Dumas were seen to have extraordinary appetites. Literature, mainly around the Goncourt brothers, is full of memories of the Magny dinners frequented by Flaubert, George Sand, Sainte-Beuve, Tourgueniev and Gautier, which were held at 9 rue Mazet, or at the Dinocheau, 16 rue Henri Monnier, or at the Dagneau, 8 rue de l'Ancienne-Comédie, whose faithful customers included Baudelaire, Monselet and Nadar.

The Louvre Museum has a cafeteria in the very heart of its own building.

On the Grands Boulevards, which were then in fashion, everyone went to La Maison dorée, 20 boulevard des Italiens, to the Café Riche (at number 16), to the Bréhant which "recuperated" the guests of the Magny, and many other restaurants that disappeared when the buildings in this quarter changed into shops and offices.

In the Saint-Germain-des-Prés quarter, the Lipp brasserie, 151 boulevard Saint-Germain, founded in 1870 by an Alsatian, Lippmann, became a key meeting place for Parisian intellectuals. Léon-Paul Fargue had his own table here, and the tiles used to decorate this restaurant came from his family's company.

Today, the relationship between food and literature is especially seen in the Drouant, place Gaillon, where each year the important Goncourt and Renaudot literary prizes are announced.

There are some very old restaurants at the Palais Royal, and the "Grand Véfour" (79 galerie de Beaujolais) is a fine example of outdated luxury. It was founded in 1740. Its guests included such famous names as Murat, Lamartine, Thiers and Mac Mahon. Next door, members of the National Convention frequented the Véry, which had been previously located at the terrasse des Feuillants. In 1808, it moved inside the arcade, to the building where Fragonard had died on August 22nd, 1806, and it was later taken over by the Grand Véfour.

In the heart of the Odéon quarter, a hotbed of

During the Second Empire, restaurants built to look like greenhouses were very popular. Here, the Brasserie des Capucines.

The success of the Poilâne bakery shows that people are returning to traditional values in their choices of food.

revolutionary activity, the Procope was founded in 1670 by a Sicilian who had come to seek his fortune in Paris. The actors of the Comédie-Française, just opposite, frequented the restaurant and "launched" it. It became one of the important meeting places of the Enlightenment. Such figures as Diderot, Danton and Desmoulins met here, and in the small rooms on the upper floor, Musset, Sand, Gautier and Balzac; then came the generation of the Symbolists: Verlaine, Laurent Tailhade and Huysmans.

The famous restaurant La Tour d'Argent is even older, it was founded in 1582. Legend has it that the use of the fork, which had been unknown up until then, began in this restaurant. It has an extraordinary view over the Île Saint-Louis and the Île de la Cité, with Notre-Dame right across from its bay windows.

The Lapérouse restaurant, 51 quai des Grands-Augustins, is another restaurant with a very old atmosphere. Maxim's, 3 rue Royale, bears witness to the Belle Époque. This was the setting of a terrible feud at the end of the 19th century, which opposed the mistresses of the nouveaux riches, who had used these restaurants as the stage for their adventures. While the summits of gourmet dining are not reached here, the sounds of champagne bottles being opened were often heard to celebrate victories of honor, as well as victories of the heart and the pompous reign of luxury and money.

The Crown Jewels

The galerie d'Apollon in the Louvre, the place Vendôme

The place Vendôme is a vast setting where the splendors of French jewelry glitter.

The crown jewels, bits of the royal treasure, can be seen in the Louvre in the beautiful galerie d'Apollon. This small gallery was rebuilt by Le Vau, after a fire in 1661. The interior decoration was handled by Le Brun, who died before it could be completed. The Académie, which occupied this gallery, had Renou, Durameau and Lagrenée le jeune work there. More work was done in 1826, and Delacroix completed the final decoration. Louis XVIII had the cast-iron door from the château de Maisons installed here. This was the most appropriate place to present collections of jewels and the treasures of the kings of France.

Jewels, objects of veneration, which depend on the complex relationships that each person has with precious stones, reign supreme at the place Vendôme which finally found its role when it was taken over by jewelers. It earned a certain symbolic value that the monarchy had not succeeded in giving it.

Some of the most famous French jewelers have their main stores here, and the capital's most prestigious windows sparkle brilliantly with the rarest of stones, and arouse the envious passersby: Morabito (at number 1), Cartier (at number 7), Chaumet (aux 10, 12), Van Cleef (at numbers 22 and 24) and Boucheron (at number 26).

The final landmark in the Paris of luxury, the Ritz hôtel (at numbers 15 and 17) was created by the person who gave it his name, and he was a friend of the famous chef Escoffier, the creator of the peach Melba, in honor of the famous singer Nellie Melba. It was at the Ritz that Marcel Proust would come to eat late at night, and at its bar that Hemingway got his impressions of a certain Paris, which was "a moveable feast".

Renovations and evolutions

Parisian urbanism today

As is the case with ancient buildings, the pediments of public buildings are used as settings for great quotes. The words of Paul Valéry are used on the palais de Chaillot.

Any city with such prestige overcomes chance and fantasy born from the accumulation of centuries by inscribing, on its very body, the tangible signs of the powers established there, of the dreams that it lives, and of the energies that conduct it towards a constant state of ideal perfection. It progressively invents its urbanization. It shatters, is reborn and shapes its appearance, creating its own seductions and magnificence by laying, on its very ground, the bases of its conquests, and of its choices. When Paris was in the hands of the monarchy, it was impossible for it to be anything other than a setting for its royal prestige. It was the French Revolution and the victory of the Republic that gave it a more original and difficult mission: it had to contain its population, and give it the more complex structures of social life. Several utopian programs attempted to make Paris a city of perfect harmony, where even its poorest inhabitants would be taken care of. The nearby surroundings and the lines of the old Thiers Fortification saw the construction of housing projects that met modern standards of comfort.

The 19th century lived with the rhythm of the cycle of the World Exhibitions that were the showcase for technological and commercial progress of a Nation which was facing a world that was becoming more and more open.

The natural site for these exhibits was the Champ de Mars, which had its own important history before it took on this role. This had been the site chosen during the Revolution to express this unity of the Nation around its new institutions.

*During the 17th century, this site was used for a soap factory and a military warehouse. The Modern Art Museum of the city of Paris was built for the World Exhibition of 1937, by the architects Dondel, Aubert, Viard and Dastuguc. Two compact wings stand behind an imposing portico of columns decorated with a bas-relief by Janniot (*The Legend of the Earth *and* The Legend of the Sea*), and in front of this is a terrace with its naiads overlooking the Seine. On the upper terrace can be seen sculptures by Bourdelle, one called* France, *and on either side of it,* Force *and* Victory.

In the variety of styles it has adopted, Parisian housing contains an anthology of the different periods of its history. The architecture of the late 19th century stands out with many beautiful examples such as those by Guimard. Here is a balcony, with a flowered arch, reaching up for the sky in Montparnasse.

Just like in a theater of dreams, a balcony near the Monceau park looks over the street with its decorative beauty. It participates in the fantasy life of the city, showing that it is an exceptional "point of view" which has often been documented in paintings (from Manet to Caillebotte).

Between the École Militaire (the Military School), this imposing example of strength incarnated in the monarchy and its army, and the Chaillot hill, the buildings of the different visiting countries were constructed. Some of these buildings remained after the end of the exhibitions. Because of this, Paris has an architecture which is strongly marked by the passage of time: from the "Noodle" style (Grand Palais, Petit Palais) to the Neoclassicism of the 1930s (Palais de Tokyo, Palais de Chaillot). The Colonial Exhibition of 1931, which took place at the porte Dorée, left behind the National Museum of African and Oceanic Art.

The ideas that guided the choices of city planners up until the Second World War remained those of the Republican origins of new power. The desire to make money considerably changed things after the ordeal of German Occupation, and the developments that take place in the ancient parts of Paris today are usually speculative operations. The charm of the past has become an expensive product. Buildings are renovated, facades are restored and maintained, but the interiors of traditional buildings are changed, and the center of Paris has become a city-museum full of expensive apartments.

The evolution of the capital has broken through the constraints developed during the 19th century, and the city has also continued its movement toward the west by creating a totally new quarter which is so modern that it is an autonomous city: this is the quarter called La Défense, with its glass-walled towers, its strict straight lines, and that final triumphal gate in the view that begins in the heart of the Louvre Palace: the Grande Arche.

When the market of Les Halles was moved to Rungis, in the suburbs of Paris, the historic center of the city was now open to developers. A highly contested project replaced the "umbrellas" built by Baltard (these were architectural masterpieces built of iron girders in the 19th century) by the "hole" of Les Halles, a tremendous shopping center, covered by a group of buildings with curved lines and false elegance.

Near la Villette, which had also lost its original role (as a slaughterhouse), the restoration of the existing buildings was much more successful and a daring new group of buildings was built to house a Museum of Music. While la Villette may have lost the atmosphere of its butchers standing at café counters, which delighted photographers such as Brassaï and Cartier-Bresson, it has gained the status of becoming an artistic quarter.

Modern art has also taken its place in what had previously been an empty lot in the center of Paris,

264

The FIAC (International Fair of Contemporary Art) was born in the ancient Bastille train station before moving to the Grand Palais, where it remained until restoration was started on this building. It is a meeting place for the most important galleries of modern art in the world, and is always the most popular artistic event of the year. Here is a sculpture by Niki de Saint-Phalle entitled "The Bird on the Arch" which was exhibited in 1993 at the FIAC.

A spectacular confrontation, as the dome of the Sacré-Cœur converses with the glass roof of the nave of the Grand Palais. These are both examples of "fin de siècle" architecture.

Built for the World Exhibition of 1900, at the same time as the Grand Palais that is across the street, the Petit Palais was designed by the architect Girault. Its monumental staircase is framed with sculptures by Injalbert and Saint-Marceaux. It has large collections of art from different periods.

The introduction of contemporary sculpture to sites adjoining ancient architecture (here the Saint-Eustache church) makes for daring artistic "effects". Far from being snubbed by the public, these are also places for children to play.

along the very old rue Saint-Martin. The daring and controversial design of the Centre Georges Pompidou, which is more familiarly called the Centre Beaubourg, Beaubourg being the name of the quarter, has become an integral part of the urban fabric of Paris, standing as a signpost and attracting an intense artistic life around it.

L'Institut du Monde Arabe (the Institute for the Arabic World), the Ministry of Finance and the Bercy Arena are the site of a new triumphal entry in the eastern part of Paris, and are works by contemporary architects. The new Bercy park is a pleasant replacement for the old wine warehouses, and it is similar to the park that was built at the site of the former Citroën factories (to the west of the capital), while the Maison de la Radio (the House of the Radio, the round building) and the Front de Seine (the new quarter built along the Seine) mark another progression of the city toward the hills of Saint-Cloud, which used to be far-off countryside.

The progressive occupation of the final free areas of Paris, taking over fallow fields, which used to accompany the development of railway lines, now favors ambitious urbanization projects (such as the Tolbiac quarter around the new Grande Bibliothèque de France, the Large Library of France). Since so many factories and workshops have left the center of Paris, there is a great deal of available land, which is immediately invaded by large buildings. These buildings often reflect the desires of modern architecture, but offer no practical solutions to the increasing problems of housing the many inhabitants of Paris. While Paris may become more beautiful and more comfortable, its population is leaving.

The Unesco Palace, the Montparnasse tower, and the Palais des Congrès are buildings that were designed more as works of art, like giant sculptures, as if a certain type of gigantic beauty bearing traces of modernism prevailed over the strictly rational ideas of social programs. Within the dynamic of this evolution, the Grand Louvre is a good example of how it is possible to renovate the past, highlight what is old, and integrate a new element (the Pyramid). But the Louvre itself is just a series of successive palaces, which bear the styles of different centuries in a miraculous unity. This is perhaps the unity of the genius that inspired it.

Page 268:
The Forum des Halles is a meeting place for people of all ages.

Page 269:
To replace the "umbrellas" designed by Baltard, and their daring iron architecture, these buildings of today's Forum des Halles, while purely decorative, play with light and transparency as well as plants. This is an urbanized garden.

From the top of the staircase that runs all along its facade, the Centre Beaubourg gives one of the best views of the center of Paris.

This was a risk, building a public building whose functional apparatus at its exterior looks incredibly modern, and this at the heart of one of the oldest quarters of Paris. Far from hiding these tubes and pipes, the building uses them as part of its decoration. Some people say it looks like a factory. The Centre Beaubourg, designed by the architects Richard Rogers and Renzo Piano, is meant to look that way. It is a temple of the culture of the century of technology. It is, itself, a portrait of this time.

Page 272:
Seen along the side, on the rue du Renard that runs behind the Centre Pompidou, it looks like a factory or a boat. It is a sort of modern ship anchored in one of the oldest quarters of Paris, which has left many traces. It is right at home here.

Page 273:
Like a work of art to be contemplated by the many crowds of visitors on the piazza in front of it, the Centre Beaubourg shows that a museum can be a site of festivity. The discovery of art can also be a game.

Among the newer buildings of contemporary Paris, the Institut du Monde Arabe (the Institute of the Arabic World), along the Seine, is one of the most interesting, because it manages to stand out in a very small space, between the menagerie in the Jardin des Plantes and the Jussieu University, on what used to be the wine market.

The architect of this building, Jean Nouvel, cleverly takes advantage of the subdued lighting that is filtered through these windows by changing its intensity and direction. This building has the temperate character of the interiors of houses in Mediterranean countries.

The Louvre Pyramid seen through the arches of one of the passages which leads to it through the old Louvre, and its majestic height rising above a floor of water surrounding it.

Page 278:
Just like La Défense, the Front de Seine quarter, designed by Fernand Pouillon among others, is a very significant anthology of the trends of contemporary architecture.

Page 279:
The frequent use of glass walls changes the perspective of a city which is in constant evolution, and which, as it grows larger, strives to become monumental and use geometric shapes. The statue of Liberty is seen in an even larger scale because it stands out so much here. Contrast is a new technique of contemporary aesthetics.

The Bercy Arena, designed by the architects Andrault, Parat and Guvan, is, together with its neighbor the Ministry of Finances, one of the greatest architectural projects of contemporary Paris. In order to build this arena, the old wine warehouses of Bercy had to be razed. Wine had been brought here along the Seine, when it was subject to excise duties. The lively commercial activity led to the building, sometimes very quickly, of small cafés and dance halls. This area was very popular on Sundays, until the middle of the 19th century, with many small restaurants built on piles along the banks of the Seine and the nearby Marne River. Similar activity occurred in the western suburbs near Chatou and La Grenouillère.

Together with the now famous Grand Stade de France in Saint-Denis, this is one of the final large architectural projects built on the space that was freed when the many factories and warehouses that were here during the 19th century became empty. The Grande Bibliothèque de France (the big new library), which takes over from the Bibliothèque Nationale in the rue de Richelieu, brings to this quarter a new form of cultural life, which had been previously concentrated only in the oldest parts of the city.

A Crown of Steel and Concrete

The boulevard périphérique

Page 282:
At the end of a shimmering carpet of water, the Grande Arche de la Défense, designed by the Danish architect Otto von Spreckelsen, extends the view which begins at the Louvre. In the central space can be seen the group by Falguière called La Défense de Paris (The Defense of Paris), *from which this quarter takes its name.*

Page 283:
The Géode, at the City of Science and Industry (designed by Adrien Fainsilber), recalls the admirable projects by the Utopian architect of the French Revolution, Claude-Nicolas Ledoux. This architecture is symbolic as well as functional.

Visiting the flea markets (here the Marché aux Puces at Saint-Ouen) was a rite as well as an initiation to the wonders of the world for the Surrealists, and they recommended this to others. André Breton brought his friends here in Nadja, *a love story which is about Paris and inspired by Paris. For Gérard Bauër, he wrote enthusiastically "melancholy: that of fate fulfilled, of novels completed, of lives interrupted. How many adventures can be seen in these "second-hand" things, which have already lived, which will live again, but will never tell of their past to their new owners".*

Every city needs gates - defensive markers, which increase the distance from the center of the city, but which become little more than a simple border. Excise duties replaced watchtowers. The walls surrounding the city were gradually torn down, but here and there they have left some subtle, silent traces, after the construction of the exterior boulevards, called the boulevards "des maréchaux" (the marshals' boulevards, because the different segments of these boulevards are named for the French marshals). Paris later surrounded itself with an express ring road as if this road marked the completion of its occupation of territory: this road is called the *boulevard périphérique*.

It squeezed its way through this area of empty fields and buildings that would be torn down, the home to marginal activity that would be displaced by its creation, and which profited a city that wanted to be healthy and have a simple shape.

Because of its shape, the rational elegance of its lines, and the materials it uses, the *boulevard périphérique* is a crown of steel and concrete.

It follows the same path as this green belt that surrounds the city that was laboriously created on the rubble of the old city walls. But it was not designed for rest and relaxation, but rather for the constant traffic that feeds the city, to direct the many cars heading for the city in a more rational direction, since this road is directly connected to the main highways which lead into and out of Paris. This road is 35 kilometers of structures, bridges, loops, interchanges and overpasses that slide into the urban fabric like a predator and mark the boundaries of the city. On the other side of this road are zones that are constantly being renovated: the near suburbs that come right up to the border of Paris. The warehouses and factories that were built in the 19th century are slowly disappearing, and their place is being taken by the most modern architecture of the entire city. These new buildings, tall and straight, with walls of glass reaching for the clouds, seem like a sort of mirror for the city that shows a reflection of the greatness that is part of its evolution and its renewal.

The Snail

From Versailles to Saint-Germain-en-Laye, the New Cities

From one end to the other, crossed by traces created by the steps of men, on geography that has now been paved over, Paris has the reassuring appearance of a snail with harmonious curls, a spiral wound around itself three times, and at its center point, opposite the colonnade of the Louvre, stands a majestic gate.

The maps in today's guidebooks highlight this particularity by giving different colors to each arrondissement as they start in the center and turn around clockwise to the outskirts of the city. This was the ultimate version (this dates back to 1860) of a constant assimilation of its peripheral towns, until the twenty arrondissements were created.

The series of city walls, some of which can still be partially seen, that defined the limits of the city through the ages, shows that this growth occurred, and stills occurs, in rings which surround the city and get larger each time. These rings protect the city too. Paris is a round city.

Surrounded by the concrete and steel of automobile traffic, the city is no longer condemned to stifle within its final limits. They are merely a step toward another limit, this one even further, and the suburbs are only a prehistory of this new limit, with their chaos and violence.

Paris has sometimes tried to break through this moving border. There is Versailles, this far-off area of lively trees and lazy statues, with its views of water and its century-old trees. Saint-Germain-en-Laye has its terraces, which offer an extraordinary view of the lively outline of the capital.

The latest newcomers to this dance are the New Cities. They bring a utopian idea of urbanism designed expressly for organized social life, planned with the best intentions of armchair philosophers. These cities are built beyond the countryside that has been damaged by urban growth, but, unfortunately, the poets did not have their say.

But there are also the highways that lead to the airports, the attics of the city, forests for walking, and parks where children can play innocently. Paris is a city that is alive.

Photo Credits

Altitude, Paris/Yann Arthus-Bertrand, pp. 11,134-135. Hoa Qui, Paris/Philippe Body, p. 126. Hoa Qui, Paris/Gérard Boutin, pp. 24, 33, 266. Hoa Qui, Paris/Jacques Bravo, pp. 29, 41, 46, 50, 52, 69 (bottom right), 110, 139, 155, 166, 174, 175, 215, 233, 245, 247, 270. Hoa Qui, Paris/Ch. Delu, p. 95. Hoa Qui, Paris/D. Derambur, pp. 128-129. Hoa Qui, Paris/J.-L. Dugast, p. 217. Hoa Qui, Paris/Sylvain Grandadam, pp. 61, 97, 99, 101, 106, 188, 280, 282. Hoa Qui, Paris/Gilles Guitard, p. 119. Hoa Qui, Paris/Icône/Châtelin, p. 143. Hoa Qui, Paris/Icône/Jean-Luc Manaud, pp. 90, 91, 165, 216, 253, 255. Hoa Qui, Paris/Icône/Martel, p. 219. Hoa Qui, Paris/Olivier Jardon, pp. 177, 230, 231, 234, 235. Hoa Qui, Paris/J.D. Joubert, pp. 147, 150, 154. Hoa Qui, Paris/Kid/Robert, pp. 242-243. Hoa Qui, Paris/ F. Latreille, p. 56. Hoa Qui, Paris/A. de Laval, p. 124. Hoa Qui, Paris/Le Rak, pp. 47, 75, 193, 210, 246. Hoa Qui, Paris/B. Machet, pp. 23, 59, 67, 76, 131, 149, 151, 167, 190-191, 200, 203, 227, 228, 262, 263. Hoa Qui, Paris/Jean-Luc Manaud, p. 164. Hoa Qui, Paris/Morand-Grahame, pp. 74, 79, 196, 201, 260-261, 281. Hoa Qui, Paris/Thierry Perrin, pp. 17, 285. Hoa Qui, Paris/Benoît Pesle, pp. 102, 103, 111, 140, 239, 274. Hoa Qui, Paris/Bruno Pérousse, p. 16. Hoa Qui, Paris/P. Poincelet, pp. 54-55. Hoa Qui, Paris/Michel Renaudeau, pp. 19, 28, 30-31, 32, 34, 35, 36, 39, 40, 42, 43, 57, 58, 60, 63, 65, 72, 73, 78, 80, 81, 83, 86, 94, 96, 108-109, 118, 121 (top left, middle left, bottom right and left), 122, 123, 136, 137, 153, 159, 163, 171, 172, 173, 179, 213, 218, 220, 229, 232, 240, 248, 249, 258, 259, 264, 267, 276. Hoa Qui, Paris/D. Repérant, pp. 4-5, 15, 82. Hoa Qui, Paris/Xavier Richer, pp. 12, 13, 14, 18, 21, 22, 25, 27, 37, 44-45, 62, 64, 68, 69 (top, bottom middle and left), 70, 71, 77, 85, 89, 93, 107, 112, 113, 114-115, 116, 117, 125, 127, 138, 141, 145, 146, 148, 152, 157, 176, 178, 182, 183, 185, 186, 187, 189, 192, 194, 195, 197, 207, 221, 222, 223, 225, 226, 241, 250, 252, 254, 256, 257, 265, 268, 269, 271, 272, 277, 279, 283, 287. Hoa Qui, Paris/Gilles Rigoulet, p. 251. Hoa Qui, Paris/Philippe Saharoff, p. 278. Hoa Qui, Paris/Stockshooter, pp. 211, 237. Hoa Qui, Paris/E. Valentin, pp. 205, 238. Hoa Qui, Paris.P. Wallet, p. 275. Hoa Qui, Paris/Buss Wojtek, 49, 98, 105, 142, 161. Hoa Qui, Paris/Alfred Wolf, pp. 10, 38, 48, 51, 53 84, 87, 88, 120, 121 (top right and middle right), 158, 160, 169, 170, 199, 209, 273. Lauros-Giraudon, Paris, p. 9. Ström, Marianne, pp. 180, 181.